TABLE OF CONTENTS

Success Strategies

This section contains a list of test-taking strategies that you may find helpful as you work through the test. By taking what you know and applying logical thought, you can maximize your chances of answering any question correctly!

It is very important to realize that every question is different and every person is different: no single strategy will work on every question, and no single strategy will work for every person. That's why we've included all of them here, so you can try them out and determine which ones work best for different types of questions and which ones work best for you.

Question Strategies

Read Carefully

Read the question and answer choices carefully. Don't miss the question because you misread the terms. You have plenty of time to read each question thoroughly and make sure you understand what is being asked. Yet a happy medium must be attained, so don't waste too much time. You must read carefully, but efficiently.

Contextual Clues

Look for contextual clues. If the question includes a word you are not familiar with, look at the immediate context for some indication of what the word might mean. Contextual clues can often give you all the information you need to decipher the meaning of an unfamiliar word. Even if you can't determine the meaning, you may be able to narrow down the possibilities enough to make a solid guess at the answer to the question.

Prefixes

If you're having trouble with a word in the question or answer choices, try dissecting it. Take advantage of every clue that the word

- 4 -

might include. Prefixes and suffixes can be a huge help. Usually they allow you to determine a basic meaning. Pre- means before, post- means after, pro - is positive, de- is negative. From prefixes and suffixes, you can get an idea of the general meaning of the word and try to put it into context.

Hedge Words

Watch out for critical hedge words, such as *likely, may, can, sometimes, often, almost, mostly, usually, generally, rarely*, and *sometimes*. Question writers insert these hedge phrases to cover every possibility. Often an answer choice will be wrong simply because it leaves no room for exception. Be on guard for answer choices that have definitive words such as *exactly* and *always*.

Switchback Words

Stay alert for *switchbacks*. These are the words and phrases frequently used to alert you to shifts in thought. The most common switchback words are *but, although*, and *however*. Others include *nevertheless, on the other hand, even though, while, in spite of, despite, regardless of*. Switchback words are important to catch because they can change the direction of the question or an answer choice.

Face Value

When in doubt, use common sense. Accept the situation in the problem at face value. Don't read too much into it. These problems will not require you to make wild assumptions. If you have to go beyond creativity and warp time or space in order to have an answer choice fit the question, then you should move on and consider the other answer choices. These are normal problems rooted in reality. The applicable relationship or explanation may not be readily apparent, but it is there for you to figure out. Use your common sense to interpret anything that isn't clear.

Answer Choice Strategies

Answer Selection

The most thorough way to pick an answer choice is to identify and eliminate wrong answers until only one is left, then confirm it is the correct answer. Sometimes an answer choice may immediately seem right, but be careful. The test writers will usually put more than one reasonable answer choice on each question, so take a second to read all of them and make sure that the other choices are not equally obvious. As long as you have time left, it is better to read every answer choice than to pick the first one that looks right without checking the others.

Answer Choice Families

An answer choice family consists of two (in rare cases, three) answer choices that are very similar in construction and cannot all be true at the same time. If you see two answer choices that are direct opposites or parallels, one of them is usually the correct answer. For instance, if one answer choice says that quantity x increases and another either says that quantity x decreases (opposite) or says that quantity y increases (parallel), then those answer choices would fall into the same family. An answer choice that doesn't match the construction of the answer choice family is more likely to be incorrect. Most questions will not have answer choice families, but when they do appear, you should be prepared to recognize them.

Eliminate Answers

Eliminate answer choices as soon as you realize they are wrong, but make sure you consider all possibilities. If you are eliminating answer choices and realize that the last one you are left with is also wrong, don't panic. Start over and consider each choice again. There may be something you missed the first time that you will realize on the second pass.

Avoid Fact Traps

Don't be distracted by an answer choice that is factually true but doesn't answer the question. You are looking for the choice that answers the question. Stay focused on what the question is asking for so you don't accidentally pick an answer that is true but incorrect. Always go back to the question and make sure the answer choice you've selected actually answers the question and is not merely a true statement.

Extreme Statements

In general, you should avoid answers that put forth extreme actions as standard practice or proclaim controversial ideas as established fact. An answer choice that states the "process should be used in certain situations, if..." is much more likely to be correct than one that states the "process should be discontinued completely." The first is a calm rational statement and doesn't even make a definitive, uncompromising stance, using a hedge word *if* to provide wiggle room, whereas the second choice is a radical idea and far more extreme.

Benchmark

As you read through the answer choices and you come across one that seems to answer the question well, mentally select that answer choice. This is not your final answer, but it's the one that will help you evaluate the other answer choices. The one that you selected is your benchmark or standard for judging each of the other answer choices. Every other answer choice must be compared to your benchmark. That choice is correct until proven otherwise by another answer choice beating it. If you find a better answer, then that one becomes your new benchmark. Once you've decided that no other choice answers the question as well as your benchmark, you have your final answer.

Predict the Answer

Before you even start looking at the answer choices, it is often best to try to predict the answer. When you come up with the answer on your own, it is easier to avoid distractions and traps because you will know exactly what to look for. The right answer choice is unlikely to be word-for-word what you came up with, but it should be a close match. Even if you are confident that you have the right answer, you should still take the time to read each option before moving on.

General Strategies

Tough Questions

If you are stumped on a problem or it appears too hard or too difficult, don't waste time. Move on! Remember though, if you can quickly check for obviously incorrect answer choices, your chances of guessing correctly are greatly improved. Before you completely give up, at least try to knock out a couple of possible answers. Eliminate what you can and then guess at the remaining answer choices before moving on.

Check Your Work

Since you will probably not know every term listed and the answer to every question, it is important that you get credit for the ones that you do know. Don't miss any questions through careless mistakes. If at all possible, try to take a second to look back over your answer selection and make sure you've selected the correct answer choice and haven't made a costly careless mistake (such as marking an answer choice that you didn't mean to mark). This quick double check should more than pay for itself in caught mistakes for the time it costs.

Pace Yourself

It's easy to be overwhelmed when you're looking at a page full of questions; your mind is confused and full of random thoughts, and the clock is ticking down faster than you would like. Calm down and maintain the pace that you have set for yourself. Especially as you get down to the last few minutes of the test, don't let the small numbers on the clock make you panic. As long as you are on track by monitoring your pace, you are guaranteed to have time for each question.

Don't Rush

It is very easy to make errors when you are in a hurry. Maintaining a fast pace in answering questions is pointless if it makes you miss questions that you would have gotten right otherwise. Test writers like to include distracting information and wrong answers that seem right. Taking a little extra time to avoid careless mistakes can make all the difference in your test score. Find a pace that allows you to be confident in the answers that you select.

Keep Moving

Panicking will not help you pass the test, so do your best to stay calm and keep moving. Taking deep breaths and going through the answer elimination steps you practiced can help to break through a stress barrier and keep your pace.

Final Notes

The combination of a solid foundation of content knowledge and the confidence that comes from practicing your plan for applying that knowledge is the key to maximizing your performance on test day. As your foundation of content knowledge is built up and strengthened, you'll find that the strategies included in this chapter become more and more effective in helping you quickly sift through the distractions and traps of the test to isolate the correct answer.

Now it's time to move on to the test content chapters of this book, but be sure to keep your goal in mind. As you read, think about how you will be able to apply this information on the test. If you've already seen sample questions for the test and you have an idea of the question format and style, try to come up with questions of your own that you can answer based on what you're reading. This will give you valuable practice applying your knowledge in the same ways you can expect to on test day.

Good luck and good studying!

Chapter 1 - Whole Numbers

In this chapter you will learn about large whole numbers. It is important to understand these concepts because you will need them throughout the rest of the book.
Here are the things you will learn about:

- Place Value

- Rounding

- Estimating

- Addition

- Subtraction

Lesson 1

Place Value 1-10,000,000

The place value of a digit is determined by where it is in a number.

Ten Millions	Millions	Hundred Thousands	Ten Thousands	Thousands	Hundreds	Tens	Ones
1	2	3	4	5	6	7	8

12,345,678

Twelve million, three hundred forty-five thousand, six hundred seventy-eight

Match the numbers below to the correct place value boxes.

1. 15,632,782 =

Ten Millions	Millions	Hundred Thousands	Ten Thousands	Thousands	Hundreds	Tens	Ones
1	5	6	3	2	7	8	2

2. 24,879,360 =

Ten Millions	Millions	Hundred Thousands	Ten Thousands	Thousands	Hundreds	Tens	Ones

3. 62,158,524 =

Ten Millions	Millions	Hundred Thousands	Ten Thousands	Thousands	Hundreds	Tens	Ones

4. 30,671,234 =

Ten Millions	Millions	Hundred Thousands	Ten Thousands	Thousands	Hundreds	Tens	Ones

5. 52,197,305 =

Ten Millions	Millions	Hundred Thousands	Ten Thousands	Thousands	Hundreds	Tens	Ones

6. 83,498,147 =

Ten Millions	Millions	Hundred Thousands	Ten Thousands	Thousands	Hundreds	Tens	Ones

Place Value 1-100,000,000

The place value of a digit is determined by where it is in a number.

Hundred Millions	Ten Millions	Millions	Hundred Thousands	Ten Thousands	Thousands	Hundreds	Tens	Ones
1	2	3	4	5	6	7	8	9

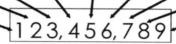

123,456,789

One hundred twenty-three million, four hundred fifty-six thousand, seven hundred eighty-nine

Match the numbers below to the correct place value boxes.

1. 748,422,719 =

Hundred Millions	Ten Millions	Millions	Hundred Thousands	Ten Thousands	Thousands	Hundreds	Tens	Ones

2. 329,608,114 =

Hundred Millions	Ten Millions	Millions	Hundred Thousands	Ten Thousands	Thousands	Hundreds	Tens	Ones

3. 124,375,277 =

Hundred Millions	Ten Millions	Millions	Hundred Thousands	Ten Thousands	Thousands	Hundreds	Tens	Ones

4. 741,588,379 =

Hundred Millions	Ten Millions	Millions	Hundred Thousands	Ten Thousands	Thousands	Hundreds	Tens	Ones

5. 504,267,332 =

Hundred Millions	Ten Millions	Millions	Hundred Thousands	Ten Thousands	Thousands	Hundreds	Tens	Ones

6. 972,114,089 =

Hundred Millions	Ten Millions	Millions	Hundred Thousands	Ten Thousands	Thousands	Hundreds	Tens	Ones

Lesson 2

Rounding up to 100,000

Round the following numbers to the nearest thousand.

1. 2,563 ____3,000____
2. 9,198 _____
3. 1,423 _____
4. 7,712 _____
5. 3,300 _____

6. 4,219 _____
7. 5,756 _____
8. 8,154 _____
9. 6,069 _____
10 1,995 _____

Round the following numbers to the nearest ten-thousand.

11. 39,092 _____
12. 19,917 _____
13. 93,254 _____
14. 56,055 _____
15. 70,856 _____

16. 77,150 _____
17. 33,809 _____
18. 35,451 _____
19. 20,901 _____
20. 48,599 _____

Round the following numbers to the nearest hundred-thousand.

21. 274,333 _____
22. 596,559 _____
23. 221,324 _____
24. 530,708 _____
25. 189,365 _____

26. 317,110 _____
27. 882,658 _____
28. 610,567 _____
29. 789,381 _____
30. 109,277 _____

Lesson 3

Building Numbers

Use what you learned about place value to sort and solve the problems below.

1. $3 + 400 + 4,000 + 20,000 + 50 =$ __24,453__

2. $50,000 + 700 + 10 + 5,000 + 8 =$ _____

3. $500 + 50 + 10,000 + 9,000 + 4 =$ _____

4. $8,000 + 100 + 30 + 2 + 20,000 =$ _____

5. $10,000 + 900 + 60 + 2,000 + 6 =$ _____

6. $90,000 + 300 + 50 + 9 + 3,000 =$ _____

7. $1 + 500 + 6,000 + 90,000 + 90 =$ _____

8. $700 + 70 + 50,000 + 6,000 + 2 =$ _____

9. $3,000 + 200 + 90 + 7 + 80,000 =$ _____

10. $5 + 900 + 7,000 + 20,000 + 10 =$ _____

11. $5,000 + 200 + 10 + 2 + 30,000 =$ _____

12. $600 + 80 + 60,000 + 2,000 + 9 =$ _____

13. $40,000 + 200 + 10 + 9,000 + 2 =$ _____

14. $9,000 + 300 + 50 + 9 + 70,000 =$ _____

15. $6 + 700 + 3,000 + 90,000 + 50 =$ _____

16. $8 + 300 + 1,000 + 40,000 + 20 =$ _____

17. $3,000 + 7 + 50 + 900 + 40,000 =$ _____

18. $100 + 60 + 10,000 + 4,000 + 1 =$ _____

19. $500 + 60 + 90,000 + 3,000 + 4 =$ _____

20. $7 + 800 + 9,000 + 30,000 + 10 =$ _____

- 14 -

Lesson 4

Estimating 1

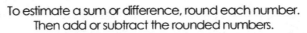

To estimate a sum or difference, round each number.
Then add or subtract the rounded numbers.

Addition:

```
  6 8 8  ⟶    7 0 0
+   2 3 1 ⟶ + 2 0 0
             ‾‾‾‾‾‾‾
               9 0 0
```

Subtraction:

```
4,0 3 1  ⟶   4,0 0 0
-  7 8 9 ⟶ -   8 0 0
             ‾‾‾‾‾‾‾‾
              3,2 0 0
```

Estimate and solve the problems below.

1.
```
  8 7 8 ⟶    9 0 0
+ 3 9 1 ⟶ + 4 0 0
           ‾‾‾‾‾‾‾
            1,3 0 0
```

2.
```
  4 6 1 ⟶
+ 5 4 0 ⟶
```

3.
```
  1 2 9 ⟶
+ 6 0 7 ⟶
```

4.
```
  3 9 9 ⟶
+ 7 3 1 ⟶
```

5.
```
  9 4 3 ⟶
- 4 9 9 ⟶
```

6.
```
  7 7 8 ⟶
- 2 0 7 ⟶
```

7.
```
  6 3 0 ⟶
- 4 5 2 ⟶
```

8.
```
  3 5 6 ⟶
- 1 7 5 ⟶
```

- 15 -

Estimating 2

To estimate a sum or difference, round each number. Then add or subtract the rounded numbers.

Estimate and solve the problems below.

1. 6,281 $\longrightarrow$
  + 3,552 $\longrightarrow$

2. 4,782 $\longrightarrow$
  + 1,321 $\longrightarrow$

3. 9,423 $\longrightarrow$
  + 6,599 $\longrightarrow$

4. 5,192 $\longrightarrow$
  + 4,807 $\longrightarrow$

5. 2,991 $\longrightarrow$
  + 5,841 $\longrightarrow$

6. 7,510 $\longrightarrow$
  + 7,291 $\longrightarrow$

7. 1,690 $\longrightarrow$
  + 4,501 $\longrightarrow$

8. 3,908 $\longrightarrow$
  + 4,687 $\longrightarrow$

9. 9,499 $\longrightarrow$
  +   532 $\longrightarrow$

10. 3,641 $\longrightarrow$
  − 2,487 $\longrightarrow$

11. 8,961 $\longrightarrow$
  − 4,540 $\longrightarrow$

12. 7,299 $\longrightarrow$
  − 5,607 $\longrightarrow$

13. 4,701 $\longrightarrow$
  − 3,112 $\longrightarrow$

14. 9,475 $\longrightarrow$
  − 7,500 $\longrightarrow$

15. 3,559 $\longrightarrow$
  − 1,890 $\longrightarrow$

16. 4,115 $\longrightarrow$
  −   805 $\longrightarrow$

17. 5,602 $\longrightarrow$
  − 2,199 $\longrightarrow$

18. 7,999 $\longrightarrow$
  − 5,999 $\longrightarrow$

Lesson 5

Addition with Regrouping

To add multiple-digit numbers together, start in the ones place and then use basic addition rules. When a number equals ten or more the first digit carries over to the next spot. This is called **regrouping**.

Step 1:	Step 2:	Step 3:	Step 4:
Add the digits in the one's column and carry over the 1 to the ten's column.	Next add the digits in the ten's column and carry over the 1 to the hundred's column.	Next add the digits in the hundred's column.	Finally, carry over the 1 from the hundred's column to the thousand's column.

Step 1:

1000's	100's	10's	1's
		1	
	7	5	9
+	5	6	4
			[3]

Step 2:

1000's	100's	10's	1's
	1	1	
	7	5	9
+	5	6	4
		[2]	3

Step 3:

1000's	100's	10's	1's
	1	1	
	7	5	9
+	5	6	4
	[3]	2	3

Step 4:

1000's	100's	10's	1's
	1	1	
	7	5	9
+	5	6	4
[1]	3	2	3

Solve the problems below. Use regrouping when needed.

1. 9 4 4
   + 2 8 1
   ‾‾‾‾‾‾‾
   1,2 2 5

2. 6 0 3
   + 4 2 1

3. 9 4 6
   + 6 3 4

4.   4 0 7
   + 3 3 5

5.   2 8 9
   + 9 7 2

6. 5 7 2
   + 5 3 9

7. 4 9 1
   + 8 6 2

8. 9 4 5
   + 6 8 7

9.   9 9 9
   + 2 3 7

10. 7 5 5
   + 6 7 5

Lesson 6

4-Digit Addition 1

Solve the problems below using regrouping.

1.   1,091
     2,157
   + 3,267

2.   9,815
       803
   + 2,216

3.   3,891
     1,259
   + 7,520

4.   2,552
     8,406
   +   271

5.   5,330
     1,211
   + 9,801

6.   4,881
     2,009
   + 1,987

7.   3,072
     1,650
   +   578

8.   1,985
     8,105
   + 1,776

9.   9,841
     2,750
   + 1,349

10.   5,400
      501
   + 3,814

11.   7,072
     6,152
   + 1,785

12.   707
     1,804
   + 2,950

13.   2,400
      962
   +   815

14.   6,074
     1,255
   + 8,079

15.   8,180
     2,755
   + 2,577

16.   9,064
     9,607
   + 6,074

17.   4,911
     2,757
   + 3,025

18.   5,787
     6,962
   + 1,570

19.   7,705
     5,321
   + 1,766

20.   3,033
     1,447
   + 9,632

4-Digit Addition 2

Solve the problems below using regrouping.

1.	4,982	2.	5,578	3.	2,121	4.	4,880	5.	6,159
	6,350		1,669		9,279		6,524		1,250
	9,811		8,902		3,364		9,967		1,975
	+ 2,652		+ 191		+ 2,127		+ 2,115		+ 9,364

6.	3,160	7.	6,890	8.	2,459	9.	6,110	10.	3,692
	9,497		1,457		9,087		993		1,157
	5,222		9,058		1,134		1,678		7,239
	+ 4,596		+ 3,126		+ 705		+ 5,157		+ 7,058

11.	4,457	12.	6,898	13.	3,070	14.	5,158	15.	4,869
	9,280		6,157		1,007		4,058		6,048
	1,170		3,309		4,911		3,982		9,263
	+ 2,357		+ 675		+ 7,963		+ 1,360		+ 2,009

16.	1,222	17.	3,089	18.	2,172	19.	3,887	20.	7,982
	1,378		6,164		4,339		3,105		3,350
	3,157		7,665		6,057		1,007		2,811
	+ 9,009		+ 5,035		+ 1,197		+ 332		+ 4,652

Lesson 7

5-Digit Addition

Solve the problems below using regrouping.

1. 54,691 10,847 + 39,116	**2.** 90,861 77,392 + 20,691	**3.** 44,388 35,512 + 64,172	**4.** 50,233 46,397 + 92,846
5. 58,732 33,020 + 12,571	**6.** 19,570 27,694 + 56,630	**7.** 90,691 51,072 + 14,321	**8.** 35,450 82,300 + 23,124
9. 60,805 84,997 + 39,111	**10.** 66,349 70,244 + 11,188	**11.** 15,000 39,289 + 2,723	**12.** 99,785 35,562 + 48,078
13. 38,058 36,298 + 57,613	**14.** 66,951 23,207 + 10,881	**15.** 47,381 61,273 + 75,507	**16.** 94,080 11,636 + 9,860
17. 39,005 29,678 + 14,567	**18.** 48,399 15,467 + 5,005	**19.** 18,222 90,309 + 66,009	**20.** 99,863 99,067 + 65,331

- 20 -

Lesson 8

6-Digit Addition

Solve the problems below using regrouping.

1.   102,220
     366,357
 + 127,475
	2. 557,365
	     166,204
	 + 254,129
		3. 325,299
		     770,351
		 + 64,658
			4. 129,195
			     632,744
			 + 335,163

5.   641,001
     237,925
 + 210,137
	6. 752,112
	     209,482
	 + 322,165
		7. 480,129
		     638,635
		 + 218,001
			8. 500,051
			     217,521
			 + 127,937

9.   637,817
     289,364
 + 123,994
	10. 491,065
	     278,605
	 + 316,221
		11. 841,316
		     958,375
		 + 175,363
			12. 150,633
			     534,110
			 + 156,925

13.   655,119
     230,754
 + 524,239
	14. 163,159
	     952,364
	 + 402,846
		15. 752,005
		     647,119
		 + 841,715
			16. 363,175
			     119,376
			 + 237,860

17.   445,123
     967,525
 + 364,129
	18. 638,117
	     500,682
	 + 438,385
		19. 781,975
		     237,105
		 + 285,367
			20. 908,129
			     117,765
			 + 637,032

Lesson 9

7-Digit Addition

Solve the problems below using regrouping.

1. 3,541,277 6,129,245 + 2,382,107	**2.** 2,711,015 3,844,362 + 1,332,745	**3.** 5,008,694 3,992,406 + 8,264,367	**4.** 8,267,200 7,164,245 + 6,277,594
5. 5,466,999 3,050,638 + 6,105,347	**6.** 7,548,007 2,215,635 + 1,365,815	**7.** 9,147,129 6,308,905 + 4,315,707	**8.** 5,113,799 5,564,002 + 6,465,355
9. 1,648,912 3,154,099 + 5,367,474	**10.** 6,905,011 4,322,966 + 3,375,378	**11.** 6,475,619 9,504,242 + 7,289,071	**12.** 1,299,151 3,637,889 + 8,652,234
13. 3,552,910 7,313,577 + 4,429,964	**14.** 6,008,799 5,027,346 + 6,244,310	**15.** 1,224,799 1,496,843 + 9,841,000	**16.** 4,208,577 5,995,685 + 5,372,129
17. 6,141,654 1,764,889 + 7,633,924	**18.** 5,639,047 6,129,885 + 3,445,369	**19.** 9,665,007 8,682,420 + 4,341,204	**20.** 5,245,895 6,636,635 + 8,547,118

Lesson 10

Subtraction with Borrowing

To subtract and borrow, start with the ones column. If the bottom number is of a greater value, you have to borrow from the next column.

Step 1: Any time the bottom number in a column is of greater value than the top number, you need to borrow.	Step 2: Borrow 10 from the next column. This reduces the 6 to 5 and increases the number in the first column from 3 to 13.	Step 3: Now we need to borrow 10 from the hundreds column. This reduces the 7 to 6 and increases the numbers in the tens column from 5 to 15.	Step 4: Now you are ready for the final step. Finish by subtracting the numbers in all the columns.
100's | 10's | 1's	100's | 10's | 1's	100's | 10's | 1's	100's | 10's | 1's
7 | 6 | 3 − 4 | 8 | 5	7 | 6̸ ⁵ | ¹3 − 4 | 8 | 5	7̸ ⁶ | 6̸ ¹⁵ | ¹3 − 4 | 8 | 5	7̸ ⁶ | 6̸ ¹⁵ | ¹3 − 4 | 8 | 5 ——————— 2 | 7 | 8

Use borrowing to solve the problems below.

1. 682
  − 239
  ——————
  443

2. 909
  − 457

3. 342
  − 199

4. 511
  − 227

5. 704
  − 165

6. 467
  − 349

7. 919
  − 58

8. 609
  − 158

9. 711
  − 459

10. 197
  − 68

11. 679
  − 388

12. 537
  − 87

13. 892
  − 604

14. 906
  − 449

15. 637
  − 205

Lesson 11

4-Digit Subtraction

 Use what you learned about borrowing to solve the problems below.

1. 6,432
   − 5,320

2. 2,675
   − 1,564

3. 4,233
   −   452

4. 5,428
   − 2,649

5. 1,995
   −   239

6. 7,321
   −   834

7. 9,211
   − 1,700

8. 3,946
   − 1,682

9. 2,463
   − 1,939

10. 8,959
    − 3,274

11. 1,295
    −   968

12. 9,942
    − 7,895

13. 7,542
    − 2,907

14. 3,649
    − 1,590

15. 9,864
    − 4,389

16. 3,888
    −   999

17. 5,001
    − 3,547

18. 1,775
    −   859

19. 3,880
    − 1,125

20. 9,567
    − 6,820

Lesson 12

5-Digit Subtraction

Use what you learned about borrowing to solve the problems below.

1. 25,911
    − 23,125

2. 40,127
    − 15,089

3. 68,956
    − 47,580

4. 42,207
    − 5,699

5. 30,113
    − 9,357

6. 92,253
    − 75,449

7. 57,115
    − 36,608

8. 21,659
    − 17,102

9. 81,678
    − 44,169

10. 47,827
    − 9,018

11. 35,157
    − 16,658

12. 50,011
    − 23,956

13. 29,368
    − 13,504

14. 48,638
    − 5,174

15. 59,239
    − 14,107

16. 66,250
    − 20,078

17. 36,754
    − 18,265

18. 54,587
    − 33,058

19. 63,017
    − 5,582

20. 92,236
    − 15,297

Lesson 13

6-Digit Subtraction

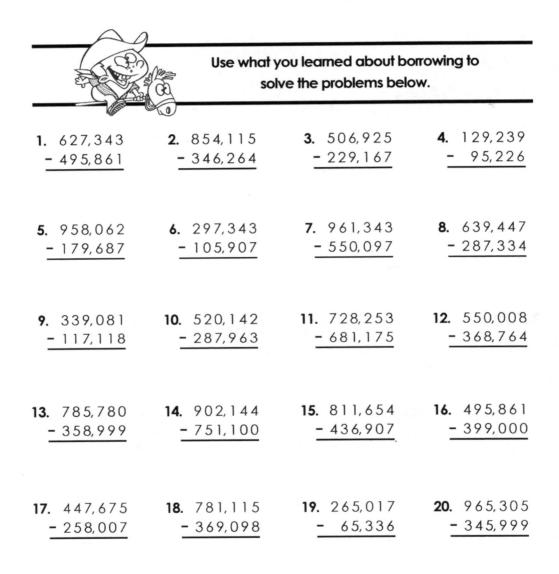

Use what you learned about borrowing to solve the problems below.

1. 627,343
    − 495,861

2. 854,115
    − 346,264

3. 506,925
    − 229,167

4. 129,239
    − 95,226

5. 958,062
    − 179,687

6. 297,343
    − 105,907

7. 961,343
    − 550,097

8. 639,447
    − 287,334

9. 339,081
    − 117,118

10. 520,142
    − 287,963

11. 728,253
    − 681,175

12. 550,008
    − 368,764

13. 785,780
    − 358,999

14. 902,144
    − 751,100

15. 811,654
    − 436,907

16. 495,861
    − 399,000

17. 447,675
    − 258,007

18. 781,115
    − 369,098

19. 265,017
    − 65,336

20. 965,305
    − 345,999

Lesson 14

7-Digit Subtraction

Use what you learned about borrowing to solve the problems below.

1. 2,135,209
   − 1,542,921

2. 4,275,394
   − 2,866,100

3. 6,429,925
   −   699,295

4. 5,985,324
   − 3,547,935

5. 7,122,956
   − 5,009,122

6. 5,588,133
   −   367,794

7. 9,002,357
   − 1,688,188

8. 8,652,116
   − 5,775,209

9. 6,339,100
   − 3,203,548

10. 9,000,142
   − 3,872,482

11. 7,125,951
   − 5,324,007

12. 5,689,008
   − 1,005,956

13. 9,958,111
   − 6,832,504

14. 7,194,926
   − 2,607,299

15. 4,305,842
   −   635,184

16. 8,965,122
   − 5,594,009

17. 6,487,070
   −   8,199

18. 9,488,267
   − 7,129,098

19. 6,125,199
   − 2.658,037

20. 5,600,204
   − 3,317,869

Lesson 15

8-Digit Subtraction

Use what you learned about borrowing to solve the problems below.

1. 32,445,311
    − 19,306,805

2. 54,009,812
    − 23,329,605

3. 72,511,420
    − 49,964,122

4. 43,652,019
    − 7,994,364

5. 17,457,333
    − 9,864,127

6. 85,674,152
    − 39,200,997

7. 55,925,321
    −   365,544

8. 90,899,425
    − 1,621,678

9. 69,129,364
    − 34,330,657

10. 84,994,657
    − 65,732,566

11. 88,299,882
    − 2,164,295

12. 39,599,635
    − 10,124,988

13. 67,290,975
    − 2,364,963

14. 50,400,991
    − 6,536,027

15. 42,633,635
    − 12,396,864

16. 95,155,964
    − 57,377,337

17. 82,112,650
    −   820,941

18. 75,644,340
    − 38,637,652

19. 59,965,122
    − 3,637,569

20. 93,050,002
    − 54,864,632

21. 66,965,362
    −   167,064

22. 92,338,674
    − 17,211,995

23. 44,294,632
    − 29,009,367

24. 84,962,366
    − 52,507,999

- 28 -

Chapter 2 - Multiplication and Exponents

Chapter 2 - Multiplication and Exponents

In this chapter you will learn about multiplication and exponents.
Here is what you will learn:

- Multiplication tables
- Multiplying 2-digit numbers
- Multiplying 3-digit numbers
- Multiplying 4-digit numbers
- Multiplying 5-digit numbers
- Understanding Exponents
- Comparing exponents
- Writing exponents

Multiplication Table

x	1	2	3	4	5	6	7	8	9	10
1	1	2	3	4	5	6	7	8	9	10
2	2	4	6	8	10	12	14	16	18	20
3	3	6	9	12	15	18	21	24	27	30
4	4	8	12	16	20	24	28	32	36	40
5	5	10	15	20	25	30	35	40	45	50
6	6	12	18	24	30	36	42	48	54	60
7	7	14	21	28	35	42	49	56	63	70
8	8	16	24	32	40	48	56	64	72	80
9	9	18	27	36	45	54	63	72	81	90
10	10	20	30	40	50	60	70	80	90	100

This is a **multiplication table**.
It shows how numbers multiply together.
The numbers in the **top row** multiply
by the numbers in the **left side row**.
Match up the rows to get your answer.

Lesson 1

Blank Multiplication Table

This is a multiplication table. Multiply the numbers in the top row by the numbers in the side row to get the product.

X	1	2	3	4	5	6	7	8	9	10
1										
2										
3										
4										
5										
6										
7										
8										
9										
10										

Multiplication Table Mix-up

X	1	2	3
1	1	2	3
2	2	4	6

This is a multiplication table. Multiply the numbers in the top row by the numbers in the side row to get the product.

1.

X	4	5	6
6			
5			
4			
3			
2			

2.

X	0	6	8	4	9
5					
4					
3					

3.

X	2	3	4	5	6
10					
11					
12					

4.

X	5	4	3
6			
5			
4			
3			
2			

Lesson 2

Multiplication

To multiply a one-digit number by a two-digit number with regrouping, start in the ones place and then use basic multiplication rules. When the number equals ten or more the first digit carries over to the next spot. This is called **regrouping**.

Step 1: Multiply the numbers in the ones column and carry the first digit over to the tens column.	Hundreds	Tens	Ones
		2	
		4	7
x			3
			1

$3 \times 7 = 21$

Step 2: Multiply the digit in at the bottom of the ones column by the digit in the tens column and add the regrouped number.	Hundreds	Tens	Ones
		2 +	
		4	7
x			3
		4	1

$4 \times 3 = 12$ Then $12 + 2 = 14$

Step 3: The one then carries over to the hundreds place.	Hundreds	Tens	Ones
		2	
		4	7
x			3
	1	4	1

Answer = 141

Solve the problems below.

1. 6 5
  x 4
  ———
  2 6 0

2. 4 9
  x 3
  ———

3. 1 2
  x 9
  ———

4. 9 2
  x 6
  ———

5. 5 7
  x 8
  ———

6. 4 9
  x 8
  ———

7. 2 9
  x 4
  ———

8. 3 2
  x 5
  ———

9. 6 8
  x 7
  ———

10. 8 3
  x 9
  ———

Lesson 3

Multiplication by 2-Digit Numbers

To multiply a two-digit number by a two-digit number, start in the ones place and then use basic multiplication and addition rules. Don't forget to use what you've learned about regrouping.

1. Multiply by the **ones** multiplier.	2. Multiply by the **tens** multiplier.	3. Add the products.

1. Multiply by the ones multiplier.

Hundreds	Tens	Ones
	2 +	
	4	6
x	2	4
1	8	4

4 is the first multiplier
$4 \times 46 = 184$

2. Multiply by the tens multiplier.

Hundreds	Tens	Ones
	1 +	
	4	6
x	2	4
1	8	4
+ 9	2	0

20 is the second multiplier
$20 \times 46 = 104$

3. Add the products.

Hundreds	Tens	Ones
	4	6
x	2	4
1	8	4
+ 9	2	0
1 1	0	4

Add the two products
$184 + 920 = 1,104$

Solve the problems below.

1.
```
    8 2
  x 2 4
  ------
    3 2 8
+ 1 6 4 0
  ------
  1,9 6 8
```

2.
```
   9 9
 x 3 2
```

3.
```
   2 7
 x 1 6
```

4.
```
   5 4
 x 3 6
```

5.
```
   7 2
 x 2 9
```

6.
```
   3 7
 x 2 8
```

7.
```
   5 5
 x 1 7
```

8.
```
   6 2
 x 3 3
```

9.
```
   9 2
 x 1 8
```

10.
```
   2 4
 x 1 2
```

Lesson 4

Multiplying 2-Digit Numbers by 2-Digit Numbers

To multiply a two-digit number by a two-digit number, start in the ones place and then use basic multiplication and addition rules. Dont forget to use what you've learned about regrouping.

Solve the problems below.

1. 49 x 1 5	2. 6 4 x 2 4	3. 5 4 x 3 6	4. 6 7 x 4 8	5. 8 5 x 6 5
6. 7 4 x 4 6	7. 8 6 x 3 9	8. 3 5 x 2 9	9. 6 8 x 4 7	10. 7 2 x 2 5
11. 5 4 x 5 4	12. 8 7 x 6 4	13. 6 2 x 4 3	14. 9 5 x 9 2	15. 4 2 x 3 9
16. 9 6 x 7 5	17. 8 4 x 1 5	18. 9 8 x 6 7	19. 7 6 x 2 8	20. 6 5 x 5 7

- 35 -

Lesson 5

Multiplication Word Problems

Use multiplication to solve the problems below.

1. If Tommy plays 7 soccer games, and he blocks 6 shots in each game, how many shots will he block?

2. Larry loves photography and takes a lot of pictures. If he takes 32 pictures a day for 20 days, how many pictures will he take?

3. James is a great painter. He can paint 3 paintings a day. If he paints for 19 days how many paintings will he have?

4. Brian eats pizza every day. If he eats 8 slices a day for 9 days how many slices of pizza will he eat?

Lesson 6

Multiplying 3-Digit Numbers by 2-Digit Numbers 1

To multiply a three-digit number by a two-digit number, start in the ones place and then use basic multiplication and addition rules. Dont forget to use what you've learned about regrouping.

Solve the problems below.

---

1. 3 2 1
x 2 3
9 6 3
+ 6 4 2 0
7,3 8 3

2. 2 5 9
x 1 9

3. 5 1 2
x 4 3

4. 4 5 9
x 3 6

5. 6 0 8
x 2 5

6. 6 4 1
x 3 9

7. 5 3 9
x 6 2

8. 2 3 5
x 2 4

9. 6 8 4
x 3 1

10. 8 4 3
x 6 4

11. 8 9 2
x 8 3

12. 3 9 9
x 9 5

13. 7 0 5
x 3 4

14. 6 3 3
x 7 9

15. 5 1 4
x 9 2

16. 4 5 5
x 9 9

17. 9 5 0
x 6 4

18. 6 9 6
x 8 2

19. 7 8 9
x 3 4

20. 8 6 5
x 9 6

Multiplying 3-Digit Numbers by 2-Digit Numbers 2

To multiply a three-digit number by a two-digit number, start in the ones place and then use basic multiplication and addition rules. Dont forget to use what you've learned about regrouping.

Solve the problems below.

1. 491
   x 52

2. 903
   x 32

3. 384
   x 94

4. 689
   x 17

5. 732
   x 57

6. 559
   x 73

7. 197
   x 44

8. 294
   x 54

9. 316
   x 29

10. 917
    x 34

11. 827
    x 12

12. 494
    x 37

13. 659
    x 96

14. 749
    x 61

15. 527
    x 72

16. 399
    x 57

17. 899
    x 75

18. 421
    x 34

19. 625
    x 84

20. 964
    x 66

Lesson 7

Multiplication Word Problems 2

Use multiplication to solve the problems below.

1. George has lots of pigs. He keeps 147 pigs in each pen. He has 23 pens. How many pigs does he have in all?

2. Penny is cooking muffins. She can cook 4 muffins per pan. She has 239 pans. How many muffins can she cook?

3. Mickey is going trick or treating. If he goes to 128 houses and collects 12 pieces of candy at each house, how much candy will Mickey have?

4. Nathan is a talented basketball player. If he scores 19 points in each of his next 32 games, how many points will he score?

Lesson 8

Multiplying 4-Digit Numbers by 2-Digit Numbers 1

To multiply a four-digit number by a two-digit number, start in the ones place and then use basic multiplication and addition rules. Don't forget to use what you've learned about regrouping.

Solve the problems below.

1. 1,491
    x   52

     2982
    + 74550

     77,532

2. 6,861
    x   15

3. 4,532
    x   37

4. 2,725
    x   93

5. 3,116
    x   29

6. 7,683
    x   49

7. 4,492
    x   66

8. 2,374
    x   97

9. 5,051
    x   31

10. 8,790
     x   29

11. 2,778
     x   86

12. 6,627
     x   61

13. 3,055
     x   57

14. 6,812
     x   89

15. 4,558
     x   64

16. 5,109
     x   51

17. 9,582
     x   75

18. 7,716
     x   68

19. 3,337
     x   35

20. 8,274
     x   59

Multiplying 4-Digit Numbers by 2-Digit Numbers 2

To multiply a four-digit number by a two-digit number, start in the ones place and then use basic multiplication and addition rules. Don't forget to use what you've learned about regrouping.

Solve the problems below.

1. 2,631
   x   12

2. 3,437
   x   20

3. 6,115
   x   25

4. 1,037
   x   31

5. 4,624
   x   29

6. 5,297
   x   33

7. 1,608
   x   37

8. 4,809
   x   47

9. 5,194
   x   10

10. 3,578
    x   36

11. 8,167
    x   57

12. 5,802
    x   66

13. 4,950
    x   42

14. 9,568
    x   67

15. 7,827
    x   74

16. 9,972
    x   27

17. 5,302
    x   37

18. 8,185
    x   97

19. 6,375
    x   88

20. 9,219
    x   96

Lesson 9

Multiplying 3-Digit Numbers by 3-Digit Numbers 1

To multiply a three-digit number by a three-digit number, start in the ones place and then use basic multiplication and addition rules. Don't forget to use what you've learned about regrouping.

Solve the problems below.

1.
```
      4 3 2
    x 3 6 5
    ─────────
      2,1 6 0
    2 5,9 2 0
+ 1 2 9,6 0 0
  ─────────────
  1 5 7,6 8 0
```

2.
```
  3 5 9
x 6 1 9
```

3.
```
  4 8 2
x 1 6 5
```

4.
```
  7 4 2
x 3 6 3
```

5.
```
  4 7 6
x 1 3 4
```

6.
```
  8 9 5
x 1 3 5
```

7.
```
  9 2 2
x 6 1 7
```

8.
```
  3 8 4
x 4 7 5
```

9.
```
  5 2 4
x 2 7 7
```

10.
```
  9 1 5
x 6 7 4
```

11.
```
  5 9 5
x 1 8 6
```

12.
```
  8 0 7
x 1 3 2
```

13.
```
  9 1 5
x 3 3 7
```

14.
```
  9 3 5
x 4 7 6
```

15.
```
  4 8 2
x 9 8 2
```

Multiplying 3-Digit Numbers by 3-Digit Numbers 2

To multiply a three-digit number by a three-digit number, start in the ones place and then use basic multiplication and addition rules. Don't forget to use what you've learned about regrouping.

Solve the problems below.

1. 367
    x 182

2. 227
    x 307

3. 521
    x 497

4. 139
    x 927

5. 865
    x 267

6. 556
    x 234

7. 682
    x 264

8. 905
    x 114

9. 946
    x 371

10. 568
    x 436

11. 637
    x 220

12. 274
    x 369

13. 857
    x 237

14. 475
    x 602

15. 552
    x 189

16. 648
    x 422

17. 592
    x 305

18. 200
    x 967

19. 637
    x 137

20. 659
    x 884

Lesson 10

Multiplying 4-Digit Numbers by 3-Digit Numbers 1

To multiply a four-digit number by a three-digit number, start in the ones place and then use basic multiplication and addition rules. Don't forget to use what you've learned about regrouping.

Solve the problems below.

1. 1,291
x 3 2 4
5 1 6 4
2 5 8 2 0
+3 8 7 3 0 0
4 1 8,2 8 4

2. 2,177
x 1 1 5

3. 4,264
x 1 3 7

4. 3,387
x 2 4 4

5. 5,189
x 3 2 0

6. 3,654
x 4 3 9

7. 5,307
x 1 4 8

8. 2,273
x 2 5 9

9. 4,892
x 3 4 1

10. 5,952
x 3 2 6

11. 6,489
x 5 6 6

12. 2,701
x 4 2 4

13. 3,119
x 1 7 8

14. 5,297
x 6 2 6

15. 9,436
x 3 3 9

16. 3,624
x 7 4 9

17. 7,117
x 5 7 2

18. 5,930
x 8 9 7

19. 8,175
x 6 8 8

20. 6,408
x 9 6 0

- 44 -

Multiplying 4-Digit Numbers by 3-Digit Numbers 2

To multiply a four-digit number by a three-digit number, start in the ones place and then use basic multiplication and addition rules. Don't forget to use what you've learned about regrouping.

Solve the problems below.

1. 6,584
   x 324

2. 3,291
   x 105

3. 8,347
   x 137

4. 4,551
   x 244

5. 9,067
   x 320

6. 6,561
   x 439

7. 7,812
   x 140

8. 3,302
   x 259

9. 5,191
   x 341

10. 4,073
    x 326

11. 8,651
    x 560

12. 3,291
    x 424

13. 5,067
    x 682

14. 5,297
    x 119

15. 9,436
    x 207

16. 3,624
    x 329

17. 7,117
    x 708

18. 5,930
    x 132

19. 8,175
    x 985

20. 6,408
    x 560

Lesson 11

Exponents 1

An **exponent** is a number that tells how many times the base is used as a factor.
It is written as a smaller number placed above and to the right of the base number.

Example:	Example:
$5^3 = 125$	$3^4 = 81$
$(5 \times 5 \times 5) = 125$	$(3 \times 3 \times 3 \times 3) = 81$
5 is the base number and 3 is the exponent	3 is the base number and 4 is the exponent

Write the exponents for each set of numbers.

1. $6 \times 6 \times 6 \times 6 = \underline{6^4}$

2. $3 \times 3 \times 3 = \underline{\quad}$

3. $5 \times 5 \times 5 = \underline{\quad}$

4. $7 \times 7 \times 7 \times 7 = \underline{\quad}$

5. $9 \times 9 \times 9 \times 9 \times 9 = \underline{\quad}$

6. $8 \times 8 \times 8 \times 8 \times 8 \times 8 = \underline{\quad}$

7. $2 \times 2 \times 2 \times 2 \times 2 \times 2 = \underline{\quad}$

8. $4 \times 4 \times 4 \times 4 = \underline{\quad}$

9. $5 \times 5 \times 5 = \underline{\quad}$

10. $6 \times 6 \times 6 \times 6 \times 6 = \underline{\quad}$

11. $7 \times 7 \times 7 \times 7 \times 7 \times 7 \times 7 = \underline{\quad}$

12. $2 \times 2 \times 2 = \underline{\quad}$

13. $3 \times 3 \times 3 \times 3 = \underline{\quad}$

14. $9 \times 9 \times 9 \times 9 \times 9 \times 9 = \underline{\quad}$

Lesson 12

Exponents 2

Write out the exponents below and solve. Use the boxes to work out the problems.

1. $9^3 = $ ___9 x 9 x 9___ $= \underline{729}$ **2.** $5^5 = $ _____ $= $ ____

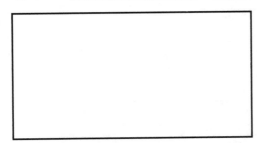 

3. $8^4 = $ _____ $= $ ____   **4.** $2^9 = $ _____ $= $ ____

5. $6^4 = $ _____ $= $ ____   **6.** $4^5 = $ _____ $= $ ____

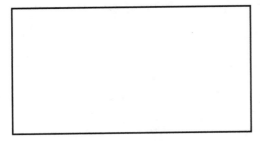

- 47 -

Lesson 13

Exponents 3

Write out the exponents below and solve. Use the boxes to work out the problems,

1. $8^2 =$ _____ = ___

2. $6^5 =$ _____ = ___

3. $7^4 =$ _____ = ___

4. $3^8 =$ _____ = ___

5. $4^3 =$ _____ = ___

6. $5^5 =$ _____ = ___

Comparing Exponents

An **exponent** is a number that tells how many times the base is used as a factor. It is written as a smaller number placed above and to the right of the base number.

Fill in the blanks to answer if each set is greater than, less than or equal.

1. 3^2 $\boxed{<}$ 2^4

2. 4^3 $\boxed{}$ 3^2

3. 2^4 $\boxed{}$ 5^2

4. 6^5 $\boxed{}$ 4^3

5. 3^3 $\boxed{}$ 5^2

6. 5^3 $\boxed{}$ 7^2

7. 8^4 $\boxed{}$ 5^3

8. 6^3 $\boxed{}$ 9^3

9. 4^4 $\boxed{}$ 8^4

10. 5^2 $\boxed{}$ 9^2

11. 7^3 $\boxed{}$ 2^2

12. 4^4 $\boxed{}$ 3^2

13. 8^3 $\boxed{}$ 4^2

14. 3^4 $\boxed{}$ 9^3

15. 6^2 $\boxed{}$ 7^2

Chapter 3 - Division

In this chapter you will learn about division of large numbers.

Here are the things you will learn:

- Understanding Division

- Division with Remainders

- Division of 2-digit numbers

- Division of 3-digit numbers

- Division of 4-digit numbers

- Division of 5-digit numbers

Division

- Division is a way to find out how many times one number is counted in another number.

- The $\div$ sign means "divided by".

- Use this symbol $\overline{)}$ to set up a division problem.

- The dividend is the larger number that is divided by the smaller number, the divisor.

- The answer of a division problem is called the quotient.

$\div$ is the symbol for division

$$6 \div 2 = 3$$

dividend   divisor   quotient

- $6 \div 2 = 3$ is read "6 divided by 2 is equal to 3".

- In $6 \div 2 = 3$, the divisor is 2, the dividend is 6 and the quotient is 3.

$\overline{)}$ is used to divide

$$2\overline{)10}^{\,5}$$

divisor   dividend   quotient

- $2\overline{)10}^{\,5}$ is read "10 divided by 2 is equal to 5".

- In $2\overline{)10}^{\,5}$, the divisor is 2, the dividend is 10 and the quotient is 5.

Lesson 1

Division with a 2-Digit Dividend 1

When dividing a **two-digit number** by a **one-digit number**, the quotient can have one or two digits. That is why it is easier to start by breaking the problem down into steps.

Estimate	Divide the tens	Bring down the ones and repeat the steps.	The answer is: **28 r 1**
$\dfrac{2}{3\overline{)85}}$	$\begin{array}{r} 2 \\ 3\overline{)85} \\ -6 \\ \hline 2 \end{array}$	$\begin{array}{r} 28 \\ 3\overline{)85} \\ -6\downarrow \\ \hline 25 \\ -24 \\ \hline 1 \end{array}$	Remember these steps:
Take a look at the first digit. Estimate how many times 3 will go into 8 without going over the number.	3 can go into 8 twice. Multiply 3 x 2 and get 6. Subtract the 6 from 8 leaving 2.	Bring down the 5 from the one's column and repeat the steps. **The remainder is 1**	1. Divide 2. Multiply 3. Subtract 4. Bring down Repeat these steps until there are no more digits to bring down.

Solve these problems. Some may not have remainders.

1. $\begin{array}{r} 16\,r\,1 \\ 6\overline{)97} \\ -6 \\ \hline 37 \\ -36 \\ \hline 1 \end{array}$

2. $5\overline{)38}$

3. $7\overline{)89}$

4. $2\overline{)91}$

4. $4\overline{)99}$

6. $3\overline{)44}$

7. $5\overline{)58}$

8. $2\overline{)67}$

Lesson 2

Division with a 2-Digit Dividend 2

Solve these problems. Some may not have remainders.

1. 5)67   2. 8)99   3. 3)53   4. 9)92

5. 2)78   6. 7)80   7. 5)73   8. 3)64

9. 4)61   10. 2)83   11. 9)97   12. 6)77

Lesson 3

Division Word Problems

Use division to solve the problems below.

1. Jerry has 24 boxes to move. He can only carry 3 boxes at a time. How many trips will he have to make to move all the boxes?

_____

2. Sandy has 15 chores to do around the house this week. If she does 3 chores a day, how many days will it take her to do all her chores?

3. Mitchell has 42 apples. He wants to divide them into 6 groups. How many apples will be in each group?

_____

4. Andy has 63 cookies in his jar that he wants to share with his friends. If he has 7 friends, how many cookies will each friend get?

_____

Lesson 4

Dividing 3-Digit Dividends by a 1-Digit Divisor 1

When dividing a larger number by a one-digit number, it is easier to start by breaking the problem down into steps.

Always remember these steps

1. Estimate
2. Divide
3. Multiply
4. Subtract
5. Compare
6. Bring down

Repeat the steps as needed

Here is an example:

Estimate	Divide the hundreds	Bring down the tens and repeat the steps.	Bring down the ones and repeat the steps.
$\begin{array}{r} 2 \\ 4\overline{)975} \end{array}$	$\begin{array}{r} 2 \\ 4\overline{)975} \\ -8 \\ \hline 1 \end{array}$	$\begin{array}{r} 24 \\ 4\overline{)975} \\ -8\downarrow \\ \hline 17 \\ -16 \\ \hline 1 \end{array}$	$\begin{array}{r} 243\,r3 \\ 4\overline{)975} \\ -8 \\ \hline 17 \\ -16 \\ \hline 15 \\ -12 \\ \hline 3 \end{array}$
Take a look at the first digit. Estimate how many times 4 will go into 9 without going over the number.	4 can go into 9 twice. Multiply 4 x 2 and get 8. Subtract the 8 from 9 leaving 1.	4 can go into 17 four times. Multiply 4 x 4 and get 16. Subtract 16 from 17 leaving 1.	The remainder is **3**

Solve these problems. Some may not have remainders.

1.
$$\begin{array}{r} 367\,r\,1 \\ 2\overline{)735} \\ -6 \\ \hline 13 \\ -12 \\ \hline 15 \\ -14 \\ \hline 1 \end{array}$$

2. $3\overline{)892}$

3. $7\overline{)938}$

Lesson 5

Dividing 3-Digit Dividends by a 1-Digit Divisor 2

Solve these problems. Some may not have remainders.

1.
```
   153r2
3)461
 - 3
   16
  -15
    11
   - 9
     2
```

2. 4)128

3. 2)392

4. 7)975

5. 9)815

6. 6)892

7. 3)564

8. 2)297

9. 3)622

10. 4)930

11. 5)556

12. 7)986

13. 2)846

14. 3)134

15. 2)408

16. 2)276

17. 3)578

18. 8)556

19. 9)681

20. 4)599

Dividing 3-Digit Dividends by a 1-Digit Divisor 3

 Solve these problems. Some may not have remainders.

1. 9)592

2. 5)344

3. 7)907

4. 2)677

5. 6)128

6. 3)750

7. 4)417

8. 8)982

9. 9)337

10. 3)827

11. 6)679

12. 2)736

13. 5)422

14. 7)175

15. 8)697

16. 9)858

17. 2)907

18. 4)335

19. 9)875

20. 5)785

Lesson 6

Dividing 4-Digit Dividends by a 1-Digit Divisor

Solve these problems. Some may not have remainders.

1. $5 \overline{)6,207}$

2. $8 \overline{)4,557}$

3. $2 \overline{)3,045}$

4. $9 \overline{)5,671}$

5. $7 \overline{)9,278}$

6. $4 \overline{)8,715}$

7. $3 \overline{)1,896}$

8. $6 \overline{)5,809}$

9. $5 \overline{)2,254}$

10. $2 \overline{)3,735}$

11. $6 \overline{)6,854}$

12. $9 \overline{)8,994}$

Lesson 7

Dividing 5-Digit Dividends by a 1-Digit Divisor 1

Solve these problems. Some may not have remainders.

1.
```
      8,447r3
  4)33,791
   -32
    1 7
    -1 6
       1 9
      -1 6
         3 1
        -2 8
           3
```

2. 3)64,872

3. 6)43,951

4. 2)89,305

5. 7)51,372

6. 5)90,139

7. 9)81,225

8. 3)54,981

9. 4)78,241

10. 7)28,356

11. 6)99,807

12. 9)70,207

Dividing 5-Digit Dividends by 1-Digit Divisor 2

 **Solve these problems. Some may not have remainders.**

1. 9)40,863

2. 6)92,025

3. 8)17,283

4. 7)59,518

5. 2)64,761

6. 5)51,909

7. 3)73,871

8. 8)81,095

9. 6)79,812

10. 4)33,299

11. 9)30,956

12. 7)99,068

Lesson 8

Division Word Problems 2

Use division to solve the problems below.

1. Reggie has 312 letters to deliver. If he delivers 6 letters an hour, how many hours will it take him to deliver all the letters?

2. Suzy is running a marathon. She needs to run 286 miles to finish. She can run 22 miles a day. How many days will it take her to finish the marathon?

3. Ray has 714 square feet of snow to shovel from his yard. He can shovel 14 square feet an hour. How many hours will it take him to shovel all the snow?

4. Dad is building a fence. He has 595 boards. It takes 5 boards to build each section of the fence. How many sections of fence can he make with the boards he has?

Lesson 9

Division with 2-Digit Divisors

When dividing a larger number by a two-digit number, it is easier to start by breaking the problem down into steps.

Here is an example:

Always remember these steps

1. Estimate
2. Divide
3. Multiply
4. Subtract
5. Compare
6. Bring down
Repeat the steps as needed

Estimate	Divide the first set.	Bring down the ones and repeat the steps.	Bring the remainder back up top.
3 24)865	3 24)865 -72 14	36 24)865 -72↓ 145 -144 1	36 r1 24)865 -72↓ 145 -144 1
Take a look at the first digits. Estimate how many times 24 will go into 86 without going over the number.	24 can go into 86 three times equaling 72. Subtract 72 from 86 leaving 14.	24 can go into 145 six times giving us 144. Subtract 144 from 145 leaving 1.	The remainder is 1

Solve these problems. Some may not have remainders.

1.
```
     21r8
31)659
  -62
   39
  -31
    8
```

2. 46)884

3. 21)429

4. 19)708

5. 38)594

6. 75)999

7. 53)864

8. 60)729

9. 91)963

10. 43)836

Lesson 10

Dividing 3-Digit Dividends by a 2-Digit Divisor

Solve these problems. Some may not have remainders.

1.
$$
\begin{array}{r}
22r5 \\
12\overline{)269} \\
-24 \\
\hline
29 \\
-24 \\
\hline
5
\end{array}
$$

2. $30\overline{)738}$

3. $22\overline{)449}$

4. $41\overline{)209}$

5. $20\overline{)861}$

6. $12\overline{)271}$

7. $45\overline{)994}$

8. $33\overline{)735}$

9. $35\overline{)755}$

10. $11\overline{)195}$

11. $29\overline{)312}$

12. $63\overline{)656}$

13. $24\overline{)681}$

14. $15\overline{)575}$

15. $20\overline{)468}$

16. $41\overline{)630}$

17. $43\overline{)129}$

18. $39\overline{)705}$

19. $51\overline{)362}$

20. $67\overline{)197}$

Lesson 11

Dividing 4-Digit Dividends by a 2-Digit Divisor

 **Solve these problems. Some may not have remainders.**

1. 13)2,691

2. 24)3,558

3. 65)8,945

4. 54)6,021

5. 41)9,278

6. 23)5,968

7. 36)7,682

8. 17)4,950

9. 44)8,962

10. 16)1,891

11. 21)3,398

12. 32)6,570

Lesson 12

Dividing 5-Digit Dividends by a 2-Digit Divisor 1

Solve these problems. Some may not have remainders.

```
        3,229r8
1. 12)38,756
      -36
        27
       -24
         35
        -24
         116
        -108
           8
```

2. 34)85,097

3. 57)96,134

4. 29)64,893

5. 45)95,507

6. 61)35,692

7. 32)96,599

8. 43)77,039

9. 59)32,072

10. 86)90,965

11. 71)80,099

12. 27)43,992

Dividing 5-Digit Dividends by a 2-Digit Divisor 2

 Solve these problems. Some may not have remainders.

1. 29)66,126   2. 18)40,834   3. 43)54,957   4. 36)37,993

5. 56)76,013   6. 84)99,957   7. 70)32,142   8. 33)33,962

9. 44)59,195   10. 91)85,809   11. 62)65,135   12. 89)99,066

Chapter 4 - Fractions

In this chapter you will learn about fractions.
Here is what you will learn:

- Understanding fractions
- Adding and subtracting fractions with common denominators
- Finding equivalent fractions using multiplication and division
- Adding and subtracting fractions with different denominators
- Reducing fractions
- Mixed numbers
- Improper fractions

Lesson 1

Adding Fractions with Common Denominators

To add fractions with common denominators, just add the numerators. The denominators will remain the same.

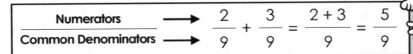

Numerators ⟶
Common Denominators ⟶
$$\frac{2}{9} + \frac{3}{9} = \frac{2+3}{9} = \frac{5}{9}$$

Add the fractions below.

1. $\dfrac{6}{15} + \dfrac{5}{15} + \dfrac{2}{15} = \dfrac{13}{15}$

2. $\dfrac{12}{37} + \dfrac{7}{37} + \dfrac{4}{37} =$ _____

3. $\dfrac{13}{80} + \dfrac{9}{80} + \dfrac{27}{80} =$ _____

4. $\dfrac{8}{109} + \dfrac{77}{109} + \dfrac{15}{109} =$ _____

5. $\dfrac{17}{64} + \dfrac{3}{64} + \dfrac{10}{64} =$ _____

6. $\dfrac{3}{21} + \dfrac{7}{21} + \dfrac{4}{21} =$ _____

7. $\dfrac{205}{865} + \dfrac{111}{865} + \dfrac{67}{865} =$ _____

8. $\dfrac{14}{55} + \dfrac{8}{55} + \dfrac{11}{55} =$ _____

9. $\dfrac{2}{13} + \dfrac{7}{13} + \dfrac{1}{13} =$ _____

10. $\dfrac{2}{74} + \dfrac{12}{74} + \dfrac{31}{74} =$ _____

11. $\dfrac{9}{250} + \dfrac{140}{250} + \dfrac{89}{250} =$ _____

12. $\dfrac{3}{94} + \dfrac{3}{94} + \dfrac{1}{94} =$ _____

Lesson 2

Subtracting Fractions with Common Denominators

To subtract fractions with common denominators, just subtract the numerators. The denominators will remain the same.

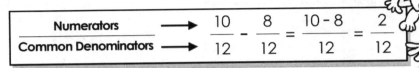

$$\text{Numerators} \longrightarrow \frac{10}{12} - \frac{8}{12} = \frac{10-8}{12} = \frac{2}{12}$$
$$\text{Common Denominators} \longrightarrow$$

Subtract the fractions below.

1. $\frac{32}{73} - \frac{11}{73} = \frac{21}{73}$

2. $\frac{12}{28} - \frac{5}{28} = $ ____

3. $\frac{78}{89} - \frac{56}{89} = $ ____

4. $\frac{112}{146} - \frac{92}{146} = $ ____

5. $\frac{233}{634} - \frac{119}{634} = $ ____

6. $\frac{8}{12} - \frac{4}{12} = $ ____

7. $\frac{608}{759} - \frac{325}{759} = $ ____

8. $\frac{45}{56} - \frac{19}{56} = $ ____

9. $\frac{178}{207} - \frac{99}{207} = $ ____

10. $\frac{30}{49} - \frac{17}{49} = $ ____

11. $\frac{246}{277} - \frac{79}{277} = $ ____

12. $\frac{439}{534} - \frac{201}{534} = $ ____

13. $\frac{77}{88} - \frac{11}{88} = $ ____

14. $\frac{68}{129} - \frac{29}{129} = $ ____

15. $\frac{894}{952} - \frac{705}{952} = $ ____

Lesson 3

Fraction Word Problems

Write the correct fractions for each question below.

1. Daryl is working on his garden. He has planted 28 plants so far. He has 13 tomato plants, 6 eggplants and 9 potato plants. Write the fraction that represents each type of plant.

Tomatoes: $\frac{13}{28}$ Eggplants: $\frac{6}{28}$ Potatoes: $\frac{9}{28}$

2. Mom's favorite hobby is bird watching. Today she saw 15 different birds. She saw 3 blue jays, 9 sparrows, 6 ducks and 1 eagle. Write the fraction that represents each set of birds.

Blue Jays: _____   Sparrows: _____   Ducks: _____   Eagles: _____

3. Johnny went fishing today and caught 17 fish. He caught 2 bass, 6 trout, 5 guppies and 4 goldfish. Write the fraction that represents each type of fish.

Bass: _____   Trout: _____   Guppies: _____   Goldfish: _____

4. Dad is barbequing for the party this afternoon. He has 76 items to cook. He is going to cook 15 hamburgers, 22 chicken wings and 39 sausages.

Hamburgers: _____   Chicken Wings: _____   Sausages: _____

Lesson 4

Equivalent Fractions

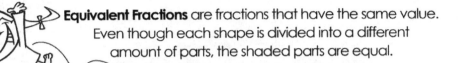 **Equivalent Fractions** are fractions that have the same value. Even though each shape is divided into a different amount of parts, the shaded parts are equal.

$\frac{2}{4}$ of the circle is shaded in. $\frac{4}{8}$ of the circle is shaded in.

$\frac{2}{4}$ and $\frac{4}{8}$ are equivalent fractions. $\frac{2}{4} = \frac{4}{8}$

Shade in the equivalent fractions on the right to equal the fractions on the left.

$\frac{1}{4}$ = $\frac{2}{8}$

$\frac{2}{4}$ = $\frac{4}{8}$

$\frac{3}{8}$ = $\frac{6}{16}$

$\frac{5}{8}$ = $\frac{10}{16}$

Lesson 5

Reducing to Equivalent Fractions

- Reducing (or simplifying) fractions means reducing a fraction to an equivalent fraction that has the smallest possible numbers.

- To do this, find the largest number that both the numerator and denominator are divisible by. Then divide both by that number.

Example 1:	Example 2:
$\dfrac{15}{21} \div \left[\dfrac{3}{3}\right] = \dfrac{5}{7}$	$\dfrac{12}{20} \div \left[\dfrac{4}{4}\right] = \dfrac{3}{5}$
$\dfrac{15}{21} = \dfrac{5}{7}$	$\dfrac{12}{20} = \dfrac{3}{5}$

Reduce the fractions to lowest terms.

1. $\dfrac{18}{27} \div \dfrac{9}{9} = \dfrac{2}{3}$

2. $\dfrac{4}{12} \div \underline{\quad} = \underline{\quad}$

3. $\dfrac{20}{35} \div \underline{\quad} = \underline{\quad}$

4. $\dfrac{9}{24} \div \underline{\quad} = \underline{\quad}$

5. $\dfrac{15}{21} \div \underline{\quad} = \underline{\quad}$

6. $\dfrac{16}{40} \div \underline{\quad} = \underline{\quad}$

7. $\dfrac{10}{25} \div \underline{\quad} = \underline{\quad}$

8. $\dfrac{16}{36} \div \underline{\quad} = \underline{\quad}$

9. $\dfrac{12}{30} \div \underline{\quad} = \underline{\quad}$

10. $\dfrac{9}{27} \div \underline{\quad} = \underline{\quad}$

11. $\dfrac{8}{14} \div \underline{\quad} = \underline{\quad}$

12. $\dfrac{16}{32} \div \underline{\quad} = \underline{\quad}$

- 72 -

Lesson 6

Reducing to Equivalent Fractions with Common Denominators

Before we can add or subtract fractions, we must make sure they have common denominators. There are two ways to do this—using multiplication or division. Let's look at division first.

$$\frac{9}{12} - \frac{1}{4}$$

In order to subtract these fractions, we must change one to an equivalent fraction with a common denominator (in this case, 4).
To change a fraction to an equivalent fraction, divide the numerator and the denominator by the same number (in this case, 3).

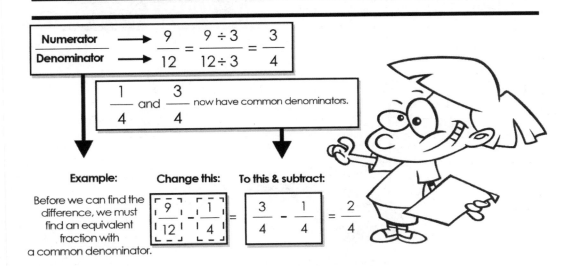

Numerator $\longrightarrow$ $\dfrac{9}{12} = \dfrac{9 \div 3}{12 \div 3} = \dfrac{3}{4}$ $\longleftarrow$ Denominator

$\dfrac{1}{4}$ and $\dfrac{3}{4}$ now have common denominators.

Example:

Before we can find the difference, we must find an equivalent fraction with a common denominator.

Change this:

$\dfrac{9}{12} - \dfrac{1}{4} =$

To this & subtract:

$\dfrac{3}{4} - \dfrac{1}{4} = \dfrac{2}{4}$

---

1. $\dfrac{6}{10} + \dfrac{1}{5} = \dfrac{3}{5} + \dfrac{1}{5} = \dfrac{4}{5}$

2. $\dfrac{8}{12} + \dfrac{1}{6} = \dfrac{}{} + \dfrac{1}{6} = \dfrac{}{}$

3. $\dfrac{9}{21} + \dfrac{2}{7} = \dfrac{}{} + \dfrac{2}{7} = \dfrac{}{}$

4. $\dfrac{12}{32} + \dfrac{3}{8} = \dfrac{}{} + \dfrac{3}{8} = \dfrac{}{}$

5. $\dfrac{15}{25} - \dfrac{1}{5} = \dfrac{}{} - \dfrac{1}{5} = \dfrac{}{}$

6. $\dfrac{15}{20} - \dfrac{1}{4} = \dfrac{}{} - \dfrac{1}{4} = \dfrac{}{}$

7. $\dfrac{25}{35} - \dfrac{3}{7} = \dfrac{}{} - \dfrac{3}{7} = \dfrac{}{}$

8. $\dfrac{32}{36} - \dfrac{4}{9} = \dfrac{}{} - \dfrac{4}{9} = \dfrac{}{}$

Lesson 7

Adding Fractions with Different Denominators - Using Division

 To add fractions with different denominators, first find a common denominator. Then add the numerators.

Solve each problem. Find each common denominator and sum.

1. $\dfrac{15}{21} = \dfrac{5}{7}$

$+ \dfrac{2}{7} = + \dfrac{2}{7}$

$\dfrac{7}{7}$

2. $\dfrac{1}{5} = \underline{}$

$+ \dfrac{8}{20} = + \underline{}$

$\underline{}$

3. $\dfrac{21}{30} = \underline{}$

$+ \dfrac{2}{10} = + \underline{}$

$\underline{}$

4. $\dfrac{10}{12} = \underline{}$

$+ \dfrac{6}{36} = + \underline{}$

$\underline{}$

5. $\dfrac{2}{9} = \underline{}$

$+ \dfrac{18}{54} = + \underline{}$

$\underline{}$

6. $\dfrac{25}{35} = \underline{}$

$+ \dfrac{2}{7} = + \underline{}$

$\underline{}$

7. $\dfrac{54}{81} = \underline{}$

$+ \dfrac{1}{9} = + \underline{}$

$\underline{}$

8. $\dfrac{27}{36} = \underline{}$

$+ \dfrac{2}{12} = + \underline{}$

$\underline{}$

9. $\dfrac{6}{7} = \underline{}$

$+ \dfrac{28}{49} = + \underline{}$

$\underline{}$

10. $\dfrac{56}{64} = \underline{}$

$+ \dfrac{1}{8} = + \underline{}$

$\underline{}$

11. $\dfrac{3}{9} = \underline{}$

$+ \dfrac{20}{36} = + \underline{}$

$\underline{}$

12. $\dfrac{81}{90} = \underline{}$

$+ \dfrac{7}{10} = + \underline{}$

$\underline{}$

- 74 -

Lesson 8

Subtracting Fractions with Different Denominators - Using Division

 To add fractions with different denominators, first find a common denominator. Then add the numerators.

Solve each problem. Find each common denominator and sum.

1.
$$\frac{12}{18} = \frac{12}{18}$$
$$-\frac{2}{9} = \frac{4}{18}$$
$$\frac{8}{18}$$

2.
$$\frac{4}{7} = \underline{}$$
$$-\frac{3}{21} = \underline{}$$
$$\underline{}$$

3.
$$\frac{7}{9} = \underline{}$$
$$-\frac{20}{45} = \underline{}$$
$$\underline{}$$

4.
$$\frac{28}{35} = \underline{}$$
$$-\frac{3}{5} = \underline{}$$
$$\underline{}$$

5.
$$\frac{3}{7} = \underline{}$$
$$-\frac{18}{63} = \underline{}$$
$$\underline{}$$

6.
$$\frac{36}{42} = \underline{}$$
$$-\frac{5}{7} = \underline{}$$
$$\underline{}$$

7.
$$\frac{81}{81} = \underline{}$$
$$-\frac{6}{9} = \underline{}$$
$$\underline{}$$

8.
$$\frac{8}{9} = \underline{}$$
$$-\frac{12}{36} = \underline{}$$
$$\underline{}$$

9.
$$\frac{6}{7} = \underline{}$$
$$-\frac{21}{49} = \underline{}$$
$$\underline{}$$

10.
$$\frac{8}{9} = \underline{}$$
$$-\frac{12}{54} = \underline{}$$
$$\underline{}$$

11.
$$\frac{5}{6} = \underline{}$$
$$-\frac{16}{48} = \underline{}$$
$$\underline{}$$

12.
$$\frac{32}{36} = \underline{}$$
$$-\frac{5}{9} = \underline{}$$
$$\underline{}$$

Lesson 9

Finding Common Denominators using Multiplication 1

Before we can add or subtract fractions, we must make sure they have common denominators. There are two ways to do this–using multiplication or division. Let's look at multiplication .

To change a fraction to an equivalent fraction, multiply the numerator and the denominator by the same number.

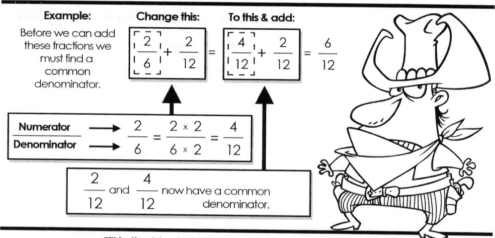

Example:
Before we can add these fractions we must find a common denominator.

Change this:
$$\frac{2}{6} + \frac{2}{12} =$$

To this & add:
$$\frac{4}{12} + \frac{2}{12} = \frac{6}{12}$$

Numerator ⟶
Denominator ⟶
$$\frac{2}{6} = \frac{2 \times 2}{6 \times 2} = \frac{4}{12}$$

$\frac{2}{12}$ and $\frac{4}{12}$ now have a common denominator.

Fill in the blanks to complete the equivalent fractions.

1. $\dfrac{2}{6} \times \dfrac{2}{2} = \dfrac{4}{12}$

2. $\dfrac{3}{5} \times \underline{\quad} = \dfrac{9}{15}$

3. $\dfrac{6}{8} \times \underline{\quad} = \dfrac{24}{32}$

4. $\dfrac{5}{7} \times \underline{\quad} = \dfrac{15}{21}$

5. $\dfrac{2}{3} \times \underline{\quad} = \dfrac{16}{24}$

6. $\dfrac{3}{4} \times \underline{\quad} = \dfrac{15}{20}$

7. $\dfrac{3}{7} \times \underline{\quad} = \dfrac{9}{21}$

8. $\dfrac{2}{6} \times \underline{\quad} = \dfrac{22}{66}$

9. $\dfrac{2}{6} \times \underline{\quad} = \dfrac{18}{54}$

Lesson 10

Finding Common Denominators Using Multiplication 2

- We just learned that one way to find **equivalent fractions** is to multiply both the numerator and denominator by the same number.

$$\frac{2}{6} = \frac{2 \times 2}{6 \times 2} = \frac{4}{12}$$ ← Numerator
← Denominator

- So this means $\dfrac{2}{6} = \dfrac{4}{12}$

$\dfrac{2}{6}$ and $\dfrac{4}{12}$ are now **equivalent fractions**.

Fill in the blanks to make the fractions below equivalent fractions.

1. $\dfrac{3}{5} = \dfrac{}{20}$

2. $\dfrac{2}{4} = \dfrac{6}{}$

3. $\dfrac{1}{2} = \dfrac{}{20}$

4. $\dfrac{6}{8} = \dfrac{30}{}$

5. $\dfrac{1}{7} = \dfrac{}{35}$

6. $\dfrac{2}{6} = \dfrac{30}{}$

7. $\dfrac{4}{5} = \dfrac{}{100}$

8. $\dfrac{2}{4} = \dfrac{}{32}$

9. $\dfrac{4}{12} = \dfrac{}{84}$

10. $\dfrac{5}{10} = \dfrac{45}{}$

11. $\dfrac{3}{7} = \dfrac{6}{}$

12. $\dfrac{3}{5} = \dfrac{33}{}$

13. $\dfrac{9}{16} = \dfrac{72}{}$

14. $\dfrac{1}{3} = \dfrac{}{45}$

15. $\dfrac{15}{25} = \dfrac{30}{}$

16. $\dfrac{16}{18} = \dfrac{}{90}$

17. $\dfrac{3}{16} = \dfrac{}{64}$

18. $\dfrac{3}{5} = \dfrac{}{25}$

19. $\dfrac{4}{6} = \dfrac{4}{}$

20. $\dfrac{2}{8} = \dfrac{4}{}$

Lesson 11

Adding Fractions with Different Denominators - Using Multiplication

 To change a fraction to an equivalent fraction, multiply the numerator and the denominator by the same number.

Fill in the blanks to find equivalent fractions, then add the fractions.

1. $\dfrac{2}{4} = \dfrac{4}{8}$

    $+\dfrac{1}{8} = +\dfrac{1}{8}$

    $\dfrac{5}{8}$

2. $\dfrac{4}{12} = \dfrac{}{12}$

    $+\dfrac{3}{6} = +\dfrac{}{12}$

3. $\dfrac{2}{7} = \dfrac{}{21}$

    $+\dfrac{5}{21} = +\dfrac{}{21}$

4. $\dfrac{4}{28} = \dfrac{}{28}$

    $+\dfrac{3}{4} = +\dfrac{}{28}$

5. $\dfrac{3}{5} = \dfrac{}{50}$

    $+\dfrac{12}{50} = +\dfrac{}{50}$

6. $\dfrac{6}{24} = \dfrac{}{24}$

    $+\dfrac{5}{8} = +\dfrac{}{24}$

7. $\dfrac{21}{48} = \dfrac{}{48}$

    $+\dfrac{2}{6} = +\dfrac{}{48}$

8. $\dfrac{5}{9} = \dfrac{}{81}$

    $+\dfrac{12}{81} = +\dfrac{}{81}$

9. $\dfrac{9}{36} = \dfrac{}{36}$

    $+\dfrac{3}{6} = +\dfrac{}{36}$

10. $\dfrac{4}{9} = \dfrac{}{63}$

    $+\dfrac{5}{63} = +\dfrac{}{63}$

11. $\dfrac{39}{72} = \dfrac{}{72}$

    $+\dfrac{3}{9} = +\dfrac{}{72}$

12. $\dfrac{17}{56} = \dfrac{}{56}$

    $+\dfrac{5}{8} = +\dfrac{}{56}$

Lesson 12

Subtracting Fractions with Different Denominators - Using Multiplication

To change a fraction to an equivalent fraction, multiply the numerator and the denominator by the same number.

Fill in the blanks to find equivalent fractions, then subtract.

1. $\dfrac{2}{4} = \dfrac{10}{20}$

    $-\dfrac{6}{20} = -\dfrac{6}{20}$

    $\dfrac{4}{20}$

2. $\dfrac{14}{15} = \dfrac{}{15}$

    $-\dfrac{4}{5} = -\dfrac{}{15}$

3. $\dfrac{13}{18} = \dfrac{}{18}$

    $-\dfrac{2}{6} = \dfrac{}{18}$

4. $\dfrac{35}{40} = \dfrac{}{40}$

    $-\dfrac{2}{4} = -\dfrac{}{40}$

5. $\dfrac{5}{6} = \dfrac{}{48}$

    $-\dfrac{29}{48} = -\dfrac{}{48}$

6. $\dfrac{16}{24} = \dfrac{}{24}$

    $-\dfrac{5}{8} = -\dfrac{}{24}$

7. $\dfrac{36}{49} = \dfrac{}{49}$

    $-\dfrac{3}{7} = -\dfrac{}{49}$

8. $\dfrac{5}{6} = \dfrac{}{54}$

    $-\dfrac{29}{54} = -\dfrac{}{54}$

9. $\dfrac{63}{81} = \dfrac{}{81}$

    $+\dfrac{6}{9} = -\dfrac{}{81}$

10. $\dfrac{54}{63} = \dfrac{}{63}$

    $-\dfrac{5}{9} = -\dfrac{}{63}$

11. $\dfrac{27}{48} = \dfrac{}{48}$

    $-\dfrac{4}{8} = -\dfrac{}{48}$

12. $\dfrac{35}{50} = \dfrac{}{100}$

    $-\dfrac{50}{100} = -\dfrac{}{100}$

Lesson 13

Mixed Numbers with Common Denominators

When we add or subtract mixed numbers with common denominators, we need to first add or subtract the fractions. Next add or subtract the whole numbers.

Example 1: $2\frac{2}{8} + 6\frac{3}{8}$

Step 1: Add the fractions	Step 2: Add the whole numbers
$2\frac{2}{8}$ $\rightarrow$ $2\frac{2}{8}$
$+6\frac{3}{8}$ $\rightarrow$ $+6\frac{3}{8}$
$\frac{5}{8}$	$8\frac{5}{8}$

Example 2: $5\frac{9}{12} - 3\frac{5}{12}$

Step 1: Subtract the fractions	Step 2: Subtract the whole numbers
$5\frac{9}{12}$ $\rightarrow$ $5\frac{9}{12}$
$-3\frac{5}{12}$ $\rightarrow$ $-3\frac{5}{12}$
$\frac{4}{12}$	$2\frac{4}{12}$

Add or subtract the mixed numbers below.

1. $3\frac{6}{12}$
    $+2\frac{4}{12}$
    $\overline{\quad}$
    $5\frac{10}{12}$

2. $5\frac{3}{9}$
    $+1\frac{1}{9}$

3. $4\frac{2}{5}$
    $+3\frac{2}{5}$

4. $1\frac{8}{23}$
    $+1\frac{12}{23}$

5. $9\frac{2}{8}$
    $+4\frac{4}{8}$

6. $6\frac{3}{15}$
    $+7\frac{7}{15}$

7. $8\frac{21}{39}$
    $+5\frac{9}{39}$

8. $3\frac{4}{10}$
    $+9\frac{5}{10}$

9. $6\frac{12}{19}$
    $-2\frac{7}{19}$

10. $8\frac{7}{8}$
    $-5\frac{2}{8}$

11. $10\frac{14}{16}$
    $-7\frac{8}{16}$

12. $14\frac{5}{6}$
    $-9\frac{1}{6}$

13. $24\frac{21}{25}$
    $-19\frac{17}{25}$

14. $36\frac{9}{10}$
    $-25\frac{8}{10}$

15. $46\frac{39}{44}$
    $-38\frac{12}{44}$

Lesson 14

Reducing Mixed Numbers with Common Denominators

- When we add or subtract mixed numbers with common denominators, first we need to add or subtract the fractions. Next add or subtract the whole numbers.
- When reducing, remember to divide by the largest number possible.

Add or subtract the mixed numbers below, then reduce to the simplest form.

1. $4\frac{3}{10}$
  $+ 1\frac{2}{10}$
  ___
  $5\frac{5}{10} = 5\frac{1}{2}$

2. $4\frac{8}{12}$
  $+ 5\frac{1}{12}$
  ___

3. $3\frac{2}{18}$
  $+ 6\frac{4}{18}$
  ___

4. $3\frac{1}{8}$
  $+ 5\frac{3}{8}$
  ___

5. $7\frac{7}{24}$
  $+ 5\frac{5}{24}$
  ___

6. $9\frac{10}{36}$
  $+ 6\frac{8}{36}$
  ___

7. $4\frac{5}{56}$
  $+ 7\frac{16}{56}$
  ___

8. $8\frac{22}{81}$
  $+ 6\frac{23}{81}$
  ___

9. $12\frac{10}{16}$
  $- 9\frac{2}{16}$
  ___

10. $17\frac{5}{12}$
  $- 5\frac{1}{12}$
  ___

11. $11\frac{21}{28}$
  $- 3\frac{7}{28}$
  ___

12. $29\frac{9}{9}$
  $-17\frac{3}{9}$
  ___

13. $48\frac{37}{42}$
  $- 9\frac{9}{42}$
  ___

14. $72\frac{25}{63}$
  $-54\frac{7}{63}$
  ___

15. $50\frac{18}{21}$
  $-25\frac{6}{21}$
  ___

16. $36\frac{32}{50}$
  $-25\frac{12}{50}$
  ___

Lesson 15

Converting Mixed Numbers

To add, subtract, multiply or divide mixed numbers by other fractions, we need to convert the mixed number to an improper fraction.

Step 1:	Step 2:	Step 3:
Multiply the whole number by the denominator.	Add the numerator to the product.	Keep the denominator the same.
$2\frac{1}{4} = \frac{2 \times 4}{4}$	$2\frac{1}{4} = \frac{2 \times 4 + 1}{4} = \frac{9}{4}$	$2\frac{1}{4} = \frac{9}{4}$

Convert each mixed number to an improper fraction.

1. $3\frac{4}{3} = \frac{13}{3}$

2. $8\frac{6}{4} = $ —

3. $2\frac{9}{2} = $ —

4. $6\frac{2}{5} = $ —

5. $9\frac{5}{10} = $ —

6. $4\frac{1}{5} = $ —

7. $3\frac{4}{7} = $ —

8. $1\frac{11}{3} = $ —

9. $5\frac{1}{5} = $ —

10. $8\frac{6}{3} = $ —

11. $4\frac{7}{5} = $ —

12. $2\frac{2}{8} = $ —

13. $9\frac{7}{5} = $ —

14. $7\frac{6}{3} = $ —

15. $6\frac{3}{11} = $ —

16. $3\frac{7}{3} = $ —

17. $1\frac{15}{22} = $ —

18. $2\frac{6}{9} = $ —

19. $8\frac{2}{4} = $ —

20. $9\frac{5}{3} = $ —

Lesson 16

Improper Fractions

Improper fractions are fractions that have a numerator greater than or equal to the denominator.	To convert an **improper fraction** into a whole number or mixed number, divide the numerator by the denominator.	When converting improper fractions, sometimes you get remainders. This means you will get **mixed numbers**. Write the remainder as a fraction with the divisor as the bottom number.
Numerator $\longrightarrow$ $\dfrac{8}{8}, \dfrac{49}{7}, \dfrac{10}{5}$ Denominator $\longrightarrow$	$\dfrac{8}{8} = 8\overline{)8}^{\,1}$ $\qquad$ $\dfrac{49}{7} = 7\overline{)49}^{\,7}$ $\dfrac{10}{5} = 5\overline{)10}^{\,2}$	$\dfrac{9}{5} = 5\overline{)9}^{\,2\frac{1}{5}}$ $\quad \dfrac{-8}{1}$

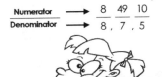 **Convert the fractions below.**

Convert these fractions to whole numbers:

1. $\dfrac{35}{5} = 7$

2. $\dfrac{12}{3} =$ _____

3. $\dfrac{24}{8} =$ _____

4. $\dfrac{27}{3} =$ _____

5. $\dfrac{48}{6} =$ _____

6. $\dfrac{93}{3} =$ _____

7. $\dfrac{25}{5} =$ _____

8. $\dfrac{84}{2} =$ _____

Convert these fractions to mixed numbers:

9. $\dfrac{15}{6} = 2\frac{3}{6}$

10. $\dfrac{10}{4} =$ _____

11. $\dfrac{7}{2} =$ _____

12. $\dfrac{19}{8} =$ _____

13. $\dfrac{23}{4} =$ _____

14. $\dfrac{26}{3} =$ _____

15. $\dfrac{50}{9} =$ _____

16. $\dfrac{46}{8} =$ _____

- 83 -

Chapter 5 - Decimals

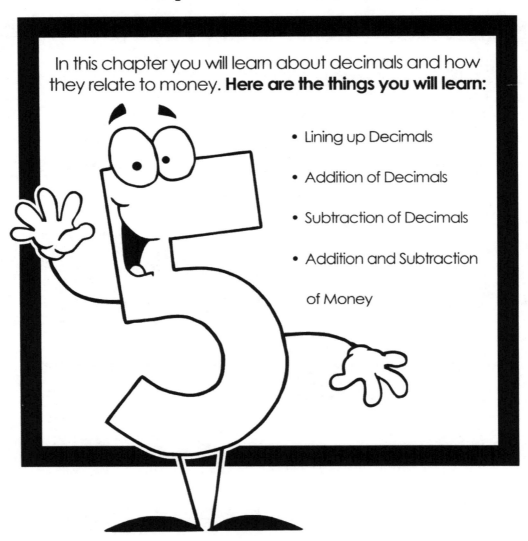

In this chapter you will learn about decimals and how they relate to money. **Here are the things you will learn:**

- Lining up Decimals

- Addition of Decimals

- Subtraction of Decimals

- Addition and Subtraction

of Money

Lesson 1

Decimal Points Addition

Adding decimals is like most normal addition. You just have to remember to line up the decimals.

Hint: Decimal points always go at the end of a whole number (3 = 3.0 or 3.00)

Example: Add 6.33, 5 and 9.5

Step 1: Line up the numbers	Step 2: Add zeros	Step 3: Find the total
6.33 5. + 9.5	6.33 5.00 + 9.50	6.33 5.00 + 9.50 20.83

Line up the numbers and solve the problems below.
Show your work in the boxes.

1: 5.84 + 1.7 + 3.29

```
    5.84
    1.70
 +  3.29
   10.83
```

2: 8.09 + 2.97 + .49

3: 6.94 + 3.07 + 7

4: 24 + 11.09 + 39.74

5: 70.05 + .95 + .38

6: 9.99 + .83 + 60.4

Lesson 2

Arranging and Adding Decimals 1

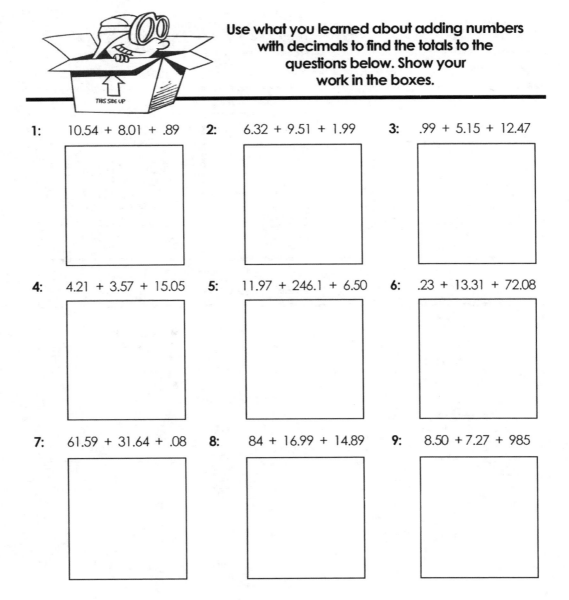

Use what you learned about adding numbers with decimals to find the totals to the questions below. Show your work in the boxes.

1: 10.54 + 8.01 + .89

2: 6.32 + 9.51 + 1.99

3: .99 + 5.15 + 12.47

4: 4.21 + 3.57 + 15.05

5: 11.97 + 246.1 + 6.50

6: .23 + 13.31 + 72.08

7: 61.59 + 31.64 + .08

8: 84 + 16.99 + 14.89

9: 8.50 + 7.27 + 985

Arranging and Adding Decimals 2

Use what you learned about adding numbers with decimals to find the totals to the questions below. Show your work in the boxes.

1: .154 + 28.46 + 11.751

2: 9.81 + .011 + 6.907

3: 3.645 + 5.707 + 99

4: 6.59 + 1.194 + 5.99

5: 29.175 + 35.19 + 3.809

6: 1.567 + 88.09 + 41.78

7: 58.079 + 44.015 + 7.09

8: 1.955 + 44.19 + 70.091

9: 9.89 + .275 + 67.001

Arranging and Adding Decimals 3

Use what you learned about adding numbers with decimals to find the totals to the questions below. Show your work in the boxes.

1: 164.99 + 805.46 + .75

2: 150.92 + 321 + 50.24

3: 95.56 + 128.7 + 9.23

4: 389.04 + 84.99 + 6.15

5: 18.56 + 991.5 + 525.09

6: 61.91 + 571.17 + 223.09

7: 7.56 + 75.61 + 756.1

8: 395.1 + 395.11 + 39.51

9: 91.8 + 9.18 + 918.8

Lesson 3

Decimal Addition Word Problems

Solve the problems below.

1. Jeremy is a great basketball player. In season one he averaged 9.3 points with 6.2 rebounds per game. In season two he averaged 24.9 points and 3.6 rebounds per game. In season three he averaged 41.2 points with 6.4 rebounds per game. What was the total of his points and rebound averages for all three seasons?

2. Randy eats way too much ice cream. He ate 1.5 ounces on Monday, 2.3 ounces on Tuesday and 3.6 ounces on Wednesday. Thursday he ate 6.9 ounces . Then on Friday he ate 4.2 ounces of ice cream. How much ice cream did Randy eat in total this week?

3. Cynthia has a parrot named Hank. Hank gets his exercise everyday by flying. On Monday he flew 5.1 miles. On Tuesday he flew 6.85 miles. On Wednesday he flew 2.97 miles. Then on Thursday he flew 4.63 miles. How many miles has Hank flown this week?

4. Dad went fishing today. The first fish he caught weighed 12.39 pounds. The second fish he caught weighed 16.05 pounds. The third fish he caught weighed 2.76 pounds. Finally the last fish he caught weighed 9.14 pounds. What is the total weight of all the fish Dad caught today?

Lesson 4

Adding Decimals 1

Find the totals below.

1.	123.47	2.	106.05	3.	253.75	4.	387.12
	34.10		23.21		73.36		49.70
+	8.36	+	1.36	+	10.15	+	6.65

5.	513.08	6.	480.21	7.	624.71	8.	945.37
	309.12		759.96		267.35		651.83
+	76.59	+	88.07	+	20.99	+	79.41

9.	11.892	10.	.937	11.	12.587	12.	67.599
	20.624		13.419		6.794		11.180
	57.393		23.757		90.725		9.413
+	8.102	+	9.144	+	24.431	+	21.924

13.	22.408	14.	18.649	15.	782.113	16.	72.399
	641.119		97.321		430.627		194.912
	36.327		531.655		67.511		381.134
+	52.176	+	944.299	+	12.549	+	26.709

17.	11.852	18.	127.537	19.	673.112	20.	587.611
	224.379		363.224		260.657		76.435
	3.991		40.916		167.320		539.907
+	921.104	+	598.644	+	6.279	+	322.621

- 90 -

Adding Decimals 2

Find the totals below.

1.	651.207	2.	300.498	3.	499.499	4.	549.339
	892.890		53.115		644.466		276.521
	509.001		88.304		320.072		155.277
	37.500		216.224		122.321		608.658
+	201.605	+	366.367	+	783.009	+	.151

5.	59.650	6.	422.231	7.	500.658	8.	684.942
	324.822		7.807		606.822		29.312
	715.155		725.237		832.615		654.697
	2.777		320.364		299.934		277.347
+	500.000	+	967.957	+	1.307	+	306.754

9.	5.001	10.	575.575	11.	229.242	12.	930.854
	470.120		53.347		301.507		292.304
	52.233		699.024		8.111		152.995
	375.032		752.990		358.999		904.654
+	960.197	+	247.367	+	295.031	+	35.002

13.	651.133	14.	865.656	15.	966.865	16.	558.715
	326.369		347.211		303.975		669.559
	959.900		122.169		288.361		781.375
	360.452		607.307		465.205		324.278
+	995.521	+	744.654	+	217.000	+	587.662

Adding Decimals 3

Find the totals below.

1.
```
   2,418.09
   4,334.49
     712.64
 +1,482.11
```

2.
```
   6,967.24
      34.13
   5,110.37
 +2,326.22
```

3.
```
   2,126.94
   3,615.03
      24.77
 +4,331.62
```

4.
```
   7,269.81
   1,382.43
     409.30
 +     3.99
```

5.
```
     604.88
   7,291.39
   3,036.13
 +9,123.24
```

6.
```
   4,168.68
   5,055.33
   4,333.07
 +  659.37
```

7.
```
   9,224.54
      75.31
       4.52
 +3,012.10
```

8.
```
     482.00
   3,312.67
   4,999.60
 +    20.54
```

9.
```
   6,287.90
     961.24
     823.36
 +2,682.48
```

10.
```
     329.58
   3,677.41
   9,003.36
 +    51.27
```

11.
```
   7,622.31
     301.02
     440.68
 +2,539.88
```

12.
```
   5,880.99
   5,951.50
      47.66
 +     9.72
```

13.
```
   4,408.12
   8,399.99
     254.17
   2,765.55
 +7,321.01
```

14.
```
      88.78
   9,100.59
      65.34
   3,036.66
 +     7.92
```

15.
```
   1,448.39
   6,691.15
   2,308.54
     279.02
 +    35.37
```

16.
```
   5,651.14
   9,842.59
   2,000.77
   2,621.22
 +2,903.00
```

Lesson 5

Decimal Points Subtraction

Subtracting decimals is like normal subtraction.
You just have to remember to line up the decimals.

Hint: Decimal points always go at the end of a whole number (6 = 6.0 or 6.00)

Example: Subtract 20.99 from 44.5

Step 1: Line up the decimals.	**Step 2:** Add zeros and borrow when needed.	**Step 3:** Subtract all the numbers.
44.5 – 20.99	3 14 4 4. 5́ ⁰0 – 20.99	3 14 4 4. 5́ ⁰0 – 20.99 23.51

Line up the decimals and solve the problems below.
Show your work in the boxes.

1. 9.25 - 4.7

```
   9.25
 - 4.70
 ------
   4.55
```

2. 30.5 - 17.05

3. 28.12 - .72

4. 605 - 45.07

5. 94.99 - 6.34

6. 339 - 40.09

Lesson 6

Arranging and Subtracting Decimals 1

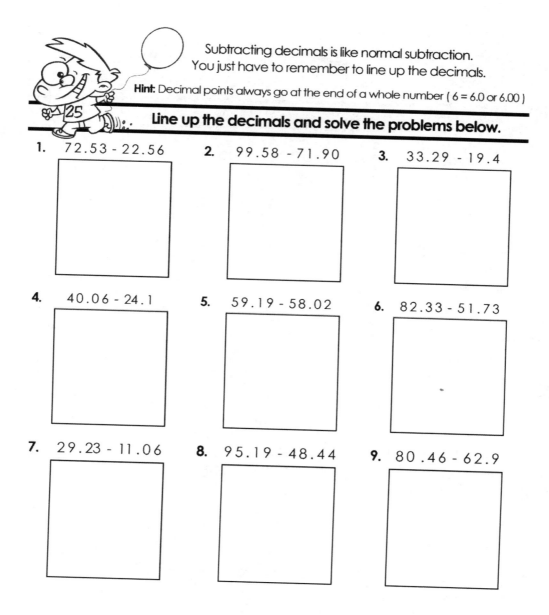

Subtracting decimals is like normal subtraction.
You just have to remember to line up the decimals.

Hint: Decimal points always go at the end of a whole number (6 = 6.0 or 6.00)

Line up the decimals and solve the problems below.

1. 72.53 - 22.56

2. 99.58 - 71.90

3. 33.29 - 19.4

4. 40.06 - 24.1

5. 59.19 - 58.02

6. 82.33 - 51.73

7. 29.23 - 11.06

8. 95.19 - 48.44

9. 80 .46 - 62.9

Arranging and Subtracting Decimals 2

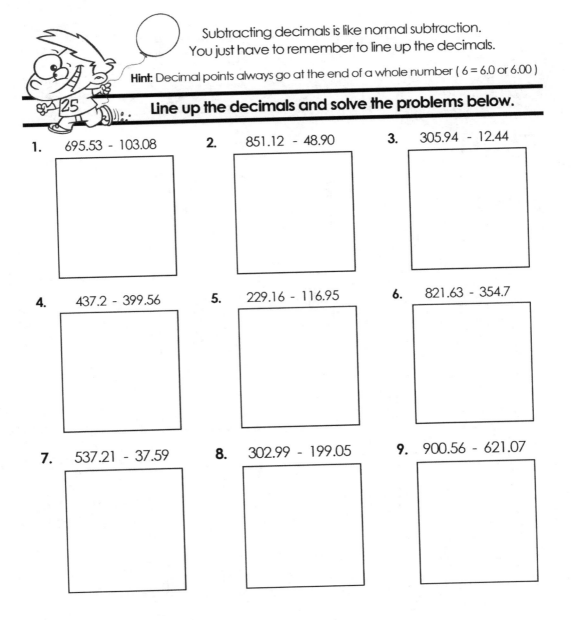

Subtracting decimals is like normal subtraction. You just have to remember to line up the decimals.

Hint: Decimal points always go at the end of a whole number (6 = 6.0 or 6.00)

Line up the decimals and solve the problems below.

1. 695.53 - 103.08

2. 851.12 - 48.90

3. 305.94 - 12.44

4. 437.2 - 399.56

5. 229.16 - 116.95

6. 821.63 - 354.7

7. 537.21 - 37.59

8. 302.99 - 199.05

9. 900.56 - 621.07

Arranging and Subtracting Decimals 3

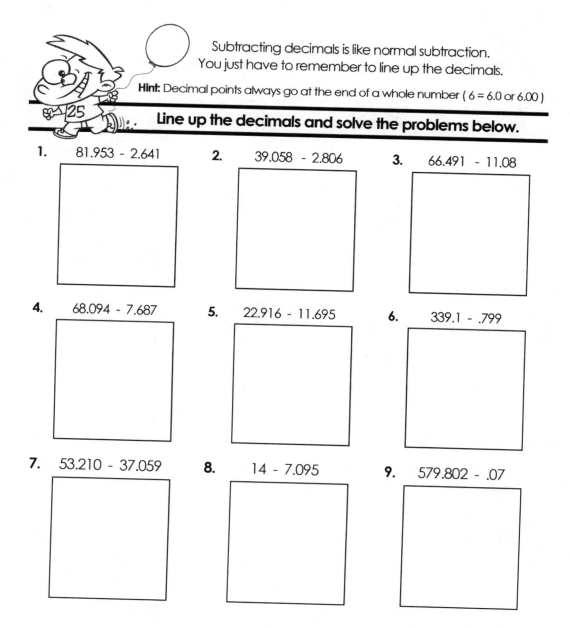

Subtracting decimals is like normal subtraction.
You just have to remember to line up the decimals.

Hint: Decimal points always go at the end of a whole number (6 = 6.0 or 6.00)

Line up the decimals and solve the problems below.

1. 81.953 - 2.641

2. 39.058 - 2.806

3. 66.491 - 11.08

4. 68.094 - 7.687

5. 22.916 - 11.695

6. 339.1 - .799

7. 53.210 - 37.059

8. 14 - 7.095

9. 579.802 - .07

Lesson 7

Subtracting Decimals 1

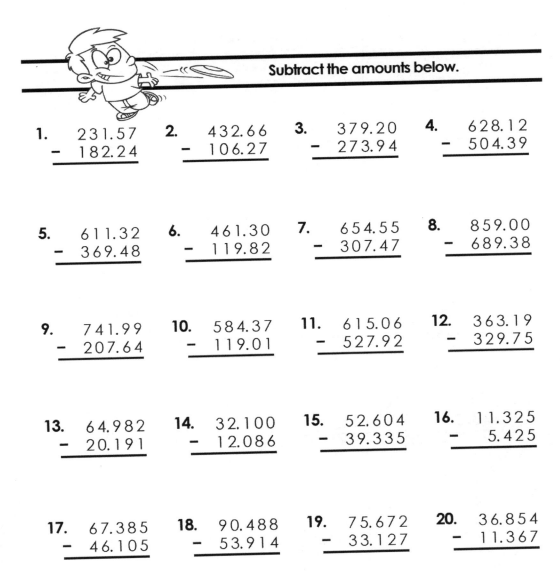

Subtract the amounts below.

1. 231.57
    − 182.24

2. 432.66
    − 106.27

3. 379.20
    − 273.94

4. 628.12
    − 504.39

5. 611.32
    − 369.48

6. 461.30
    − 119.82

7. 654.55
    − 307.47

8. 859.00
    − 689.38

9. 741.99
    − 207.64

10. 584.37
    − 119.01

11. 615.06
    − 527.92

12. 363.19
    − 329.75

13. 64.982
    − 20.191

14. 32.100
    − 12.086

15. 52.604
    − 39.335

16. 11.325
    − 5.425

17. 67.385
    − 46.105

18. 90.488
    − 53.914

19. 75.672
    − 33.127

20. 36.854
    − 11.367

Subtracting Decimals 2

Subtract the amounts below.

1. 1,334.62
    − 451.39

2. 2,485.12
    − 384.67

3. 4,645.14
    − 185.33

4. 3,313.74
    − 599.91

5. 5,482.49
    − 420.24

6. 7,893.72
    − 599.32

7. 6,820.47
    − 875.97

8. 2,339.00
    − 922.11

9. 5,894.27
    −3,554.72

10. 8,775.54
    −3,997.32

11. 7,654.41
    −5,229.80

12. 9,501.64
    −8,329.33

13. 628.399
    −175.508

14. 977.687
    − 345.113

15. 710.910
    − 84.456

16. 527.842
    − 211.611

17. 139.209
    − 44.364

18. 374.346
    −171.712

19. 452.833
    − 299.425

20. 926.001
    −364.967

Subtracting Decimals 3

Subtract the amounts below.

1. 49.9262
    − 32.6139

2. 69.8420
    − 29.9609

3. 39.7124
    − 18.2570

4. 84.4962
    − 38.8691

5. 720.581
    − 556.512

6. 521.003
    − 352.109

7. 120.589
    − 100.075

8. 264.892
    − 155.684

9. 49,078.2
    − 38,865.1

10. 8,009.01
    − 6,420.57

11. 9,569.25
    − 3,365.72

12. 7.65940
    − 2.29995

13. 3,965.21
    − 1,788.95

14. 548.722
    − 345.871

15. 2.99265
    − .95846

16. 90.0364
    − 77.8205

17. 89,756.1
    − 15,672.7

18. 77,582.1
    − 56,963.8

19. 33,587.2
    − 19,985.7

20. 9,987.02
    − 8,908.25

Lesson 8

Decimal Subtraction Word Problems

Solve the problems below.

1. Mike needs to swim 6 miles a week to get strong enough to make the swim team. On Monday he swam 1.34 miles. On Tuesday he swam 2.49 miles. On Wednesday he swam .82 miles. How much further must he swim to reach his goal of 6 miles?

2. Jenny wants to lift 100 pounds of weight each day. First she lifted 10.57 pounds, then she lifted 29.96 pounds. Next she lifted 32.65 pounds. How much more weight does she need to lift to reach her goal?

3. Newt needs a total of 300 points on his school projects to go on the field trip. On the first project he scored 86.57 points. On the second project he scored 95.36 points. On the next project he scored 64.11 points. How many more points must he score to go on the trip?

4. James was using so much water playing in the sprinkler that his mom set a limit of 15 gallons per week. On the first day he used 2.65 gallons. On the second day he used 3.21 gallons. On the third day James used 4.81 gallons. Then on the fourth day he used 1.92 gallons. How much water does James have left this week?

- 100 -

Lesson 9

Adding Money 1

The rules that we learned for adding decimals is also how we add money.

289.64	$289.64
+ 56.11 =	+ $56.11
345.75	$345.75

Find the totals below.

1. $103.32
    + $49.08
    $152.40

2. $315.15
    + $12.99

3. $91.64
    + $296.12

4. $144.75
    + $82.32

5. $257.95
    + $189.05

6. $642.44
    + $791.17

7. $309.37
    + $276.24

8. $914.70
    + $367.05

9. $454.12
    $59.99
    + $375.36

10. $708.51
    $623.78
    + $11.63

11. $34.33
    $551.40
    + $186.17

12. $691.11
    $320.95
    + $64.32

13. $111.88
    $965.42
    + $375.30

14. $399.23
    $499.67
    + $233.99

15. $607.14
    $324.24
    + $178.17

16. $119.67
    $394.66
    + $367.92

Adding Money 2

Find the totals below.

1. $108.22
   $399.08
   + $12.28
   _____

2. $56.44
   $275.17
   + $2.36
   _____

3. $480.55
   $59.63
   + $237.11
   _____

4. $365.99
   $264.56
   + $12.00
   _____

5. $564.23
   $257.67
   + $106.63
   _____

6. $216.21
   $347.96
   + $964.07
   _____

7. $754.55
   $191.19
   + $267.67
   _____

8. $908.09
   $124.64
   + $573.11
   _____

9. $245.77
   $331.06
   $24.33
   + $100.97
   _____

10. $210.11
    $772.72
    $186.80
    + $67.29
    _____

11. $662.95
    $97.84
    $205.04
    + $177.00
    _____

12. $302.34
    $475.62
    $65.24
    + $134.89
    _____

13. $905.15
    $465.55
    $992.61
    + $133.21
    _____

14. $488.88
    $706.11
    $300.37
    + $511.77
    _____

15. $625.33
    $233.31
    $914.45
    + $928.17
    _____

16. $723.99
    $949.12
    $811.34
    + $267.09
    _____

17. $635.01
    $199.11
    $208.28
    + $322.37
    _____

18. $500.49
    $1.11
    $600.59
    + $37.64
    _____

19. $368.84
    $675.64
    $99.30
    + $261.71
    _____

20. $299.02
    $103.65
    $690.31
    + $782.57
    _____

- 102 -

Lesson 10

Subtracting Money 1

Now that you know how to subtract decimals, use what you've learned to answer these money problems.

15.63	$15.63
− 2.12 =	− $ 2.12
13.51	$13.51

Subtract the amounts below.

1. $6.22
   − $3.84
   $2.38

2. $4.70
   − $1.35

3. $3.84
   − $1.99

4. $7.79
   − $5.32

5. $8.84
   − $3.53

6. $6.85
   − $5.06

7. $9.98
   − $6.16

8. $9.27
   − $4.64

9. $8.99
   − $6.13

10. $3.08
   − $.94

11. $7.12
   − $5.37

12. $6.39
   − $2.17

13. $135.07
   − $75.98

14. $209.47
   − $105.12

15. $466.17
   − $389.55

16. $349.68
   − $127.35

17. $859.07
   − $407.98

18. $654.00
   − $332.37

19. $567.25
   − $125.74

20. $804.91
   − $722.05

Subtracting Money 2

Subtract the amounts below.

1. $275.29
   - $107.72

2. $535.11
   - $299.39

3. $332.88
   - $111.49

4. $630.00
   - $424.84

5. $643.17
   - $307.51

6. $800.99
   - $115.35

7. $772.63
   - $631.51

8. $704.90
   - $639.17

9. $551.12
   - $337.94

10. $675.99
   - $167.91

11. $240.11
   - $177.54

12. $999.00
   - $327.29

13. $490.17
   - $215.05

14. $807.00
   - $318.37

15. $420.34
   - $385.94

16. $788.40
   - $264.19

17. $711.72
   - $499.07

18. $470.97
   - $295.48

19. $849.84
   - $601.31

20. $511.31
   - $294.52

Lesson 11

Decimal Points Multiplication

To multiply decimals, start by multiplying the numbers just as if they were whole numbers.

Example: Multiply 4.22 by 3.5

Step 1:
Line up the numbers on the right - **do not align the decimal points.**

```
  4.22
x  3.5
```

Step 2:
Starting on the right, multiply each digit in the top number by each digit in the bottom number, just as with whole numbers. Then add the products.

```
   4.22
x   3.5
   2110
+12660
  14770
```

Step 3:
Place the decimal point in the answer by starting at the right and moving the number of places equal to the sum of the decimal places in both numbers multiplied.

```
   4.22  ← 2 decimal places
x   3.5  ← 1 decimal place
   2110
+12660
  14.770  ← 3 decimal places
```

Multiply the problems below and correctly align the decimals.

1. 8.3
x 6.4
```
  332
+4980
53.12
```

2. 3.3
x 2.9

3. 6.7
x 4.4

4. 5.9
x 3.6

5. 4.5
x 2.9

6. 8.5
x 6.7

7. 4.9
x 2.7

8. 9.8
x 6.2

9. 7.7
x 5.8

10. 9.5
x 8.2

11. 8.8
x 7.4

12. 5.9
x 5.7

13. 6.2
x 4.9

14. 4.3
x 2.5

15. 8.7
x 3.9

Lesson 12

Multiplying Decimals 1

Multiply the problems below and correctly align the decimals.

1. 4.2 9
    x   5.3
    ─────────
    2 2.7 3 7

2. 6.8 5
    x .8 6
    ─────────

3. 3.4 2
    x   1.3
    ─────────

4. 5.3 7
    x   6.4
    ─────────

5. 7.3 2
    x   2.6
    ─────────

6. 8 5.5
    x   .3 2
    ─────────

7. 6 3.1
    x   .5 6
    ─────────

8. 2 9.4
    x   4 9
    ─────────

9. 9.9 9
    x .8 3
    ─────────

10. 6 7.2
     x   2.9
     ─────────

11. .2 4 9
     x   .9 7
     ─────────

12. 4 3.3
     x   2 3
     ─────────

13. 5 5.3
     x .5 8
     ─────────

14. 6 8.2
     x   4.3
     ─────────

15. .9 2 7
     x   7.2
     ─────────

16. 7 7.3
     x   2.4
     ─────────

17. 2.4 5
     x .8 4
     ─────────

18. 8 2.7
     x   2.7
     ─────────

19. 5 6.6
     x   9 9
     ─────────

20. 6.0 8
     x .6 7
     ─────────

21. 8.5 2
     x   3.7
     ─────────

22. 5 9.9
     x   6.6
     ─────────

23. 2.8 7
     x   9.4
     ─────────

24. 3 6.2
     x .5 5
     ─────────

25. 9.0 4
     x   4 9
     ─────────

Multiplying Decimals 2

Multiply the problems below and correctly align the decimals.

1. 1 8.3 2
    x   6.8
    _____

2. 4 4.0 9
    x   .3 3
    _____

3. 2 2.3 9
    x   7 4
    _____

4. 5 7.8 2
    x   2.9
    _____

5. 7 7.3 2
    x   .5 5
    _____

6. 3.4 4 7
    x   4.1
    _____

7. 5.7 7 2
    x   5 9
    _____

8. 3 3.4 7
    x   3.3
    _____

9. 6 6 2.5
    x   1.4
    _____

10. 4.2 6 2
    x   5.7
    _____

11. 8 2 9 9
    x   .8 8
    _____

12. 4 2 9.8
    x   4.1
    _____

13. 5.7 2 3
    x   6 3
    _____

14. 8 6 4.1
    x   .5 9
    _____

15. 9 3.2 2
    x   2.9
    _____

16. 7.0 8 5
    x   3 7
    _____

17. 3 6 7.5
    x   4.5
    _____

18. 9 4.4 7
    x   .8 3
    _____

19. 7.2 4 5
    x   7.6
    _____

20. 3 2.6 4
    x   5.9
    _____

21. 9 9 5.3
    x   8.4
    _____

22. 8 1 2 7
    x   .9 9
    _____

23. 5.3 3 3
    x   6.6
    _____

24. 8 1.2 4
    x   .3 4
    _____

25. 9 6.7 7
    x   7.7
    _____

Multiplying Decimals 3

1. 2 3 9.4
   x 3.9 2

2. 7.8 6 3
   x   4 5.5

3. 5 3.2 2
   x   8.4 5

4. 4.9 7 7
   x .3 6 8

5. 3 6 9.9
   x   1 5.4

6. 2 3.1 8
   x   5 3.6

7. 9 4 6.2
   x .3 3 7

8. 4.5 5 6
   x   6 6.8

9. 3 2 7.4
   x   4.1 9

10. 5.5 8 5
    x 7 2.5

11. .7 2 6 9
    x   3 4 2

12. 4 6 5.7
    x   5 9.9

13. 3.6 9 7
    x   2 3.5

14. 2 2.4 2
    x 8.2 9

15. 6.8 2 3
    x   3 7.7

16. 5 9 3.7
    x   9 2.5

17. 7.5 5 7
    x 8 2.7

18. 9 5 2.9
    x   6.3 4

19. 3.6 6 9
    x 2 9.2

20. 5 2 4 7
    x   7.9 4

Chapter 6 - Geometry

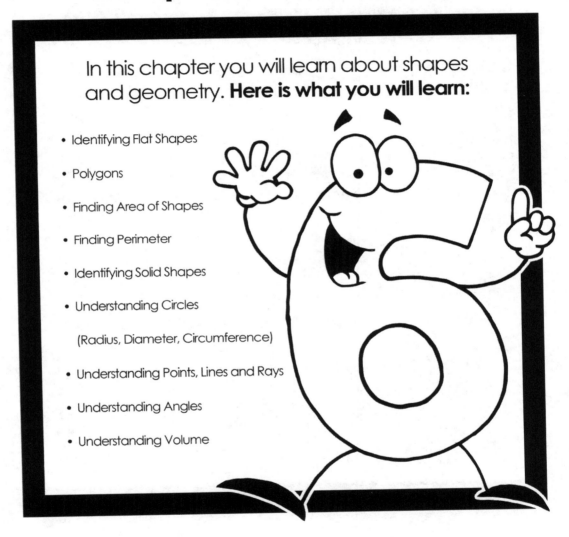

In this chapter you will learn about shapes and geometry. **Here is what you will learn:**

- Identifying Flat Shapes

- Polygons

- Finding Area of Shapes

- Finding Perimeter

- Identifying Solid Shapes

- Understanding Circles

  (Radius, Diameter, Circumference)

- Understanding Points, Lines and Rays

- Understanding Angles

- Understanding Volume

Flat Shapes

Shapes can come in any size and can have many sides. Here are the flat shapes you will learn about in this chapter.

Circle
(1 side)

Triangle
(3 sides)

Rectangle
(4 sides)

Square
(4 sides)

Rhombus
(4 sides)

Parallelogram
(4 sides)

Trapezoid
(4 sides)

Pentagon
(5 sides)

Hexagon
(6 sides)

Heptagon
(7 sides)

Octagon
(8 sides)

Nonagon
(9 sides)

Decagon
(10 sides)

Lesson 1

Understanding Polygons

- A **polygon** is a closed plane figure made up of 3 or more line segments.
- Polygons that have all sides of equal length are called regular polygons.
- Polygons are named depending on the number of lines that form their boundaries.

Here are some examples of **polygons**:

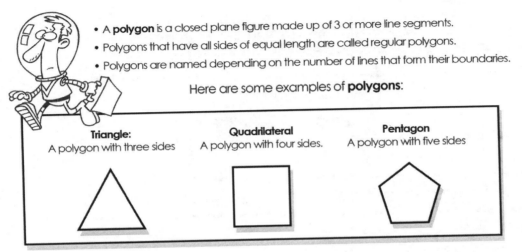

Triangle:
A polygon with three sides

Quadrilateral
A polygon with four sides.

Pentagon
A polygon with five sides

A **quadrilateral** is a four-sided polygon. Here are some types of **quadrilateral** shapes:

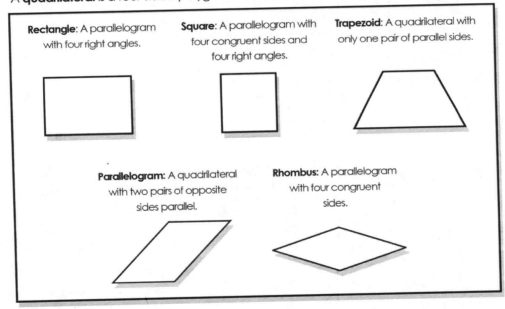

Rectangle: A parallelogram with four right angles.

Square: A parallelogram with four congruent sides and four right angles.

Trapezoid: A quadrilateral with only one pair of parallel sides.

Parallelogram: A quadrilateral with two pairs of opposite sides parallel.

Rhombus: A parallelogram with four congruent sides.

Lesson 2

Finding Area of Squares and Rectangles

Area is the measurement of a shape's surface area.
To find the **area** of a square, multiply the length by the width.

109 ft.

44 ft.

Area = 109 ft. x 44 ft. = 4,796 ft.^{2}
Area = 4,796 ft.^{2}

Find the area of each shape. Write the problem out.

1. 74 in.

74 in.

74in. x 74in. = 5,476 in.^{2}

2. 134 ft.

749 ft.

3.

205 in.   205 in.

4. 299 ft.

436 ft.

5. 637 in.

637 in.

6. 1,262 yd.

507 yd.

Lesson 3

Finding Area of Triangles

To find the **area** of a **triangle** use the formula below:

Area = $\frac{1}{2}$ of base x height

Area = 14in. x 8in. ÷ 2 = 56 in.^{2}

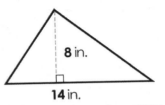

8 in.

14 in.

Find the area of each triangle. Write the problem out.

1.

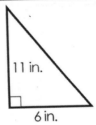

11 in.

6 in.

2.

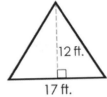

12 ft.

17 ft.

3.

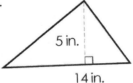

5 in.

14 in.

11in. x 6in. ÷ 2 = 33 in.^{2}

4.

75 in.

46 in.

5.

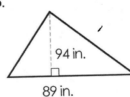

94 in.

89 in.

6.

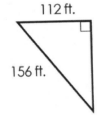

112 ft.

156 ft.

- 113 -

Lesson 4

Finding Area of Parallelograms

To find the area of a parallelogram use what we learned before and multiply height times width.

Area = 12 ft. x 9 ft. = 108 ft.^{2}

Area = 108 ft.^{2}

Find the area of each parallelogram. Write the problem out.

1.

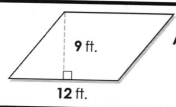

6 ft.

6 ft.

2.

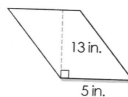

13 in.

5 in.

3.

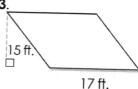

15 ft.

17 ft.

6 ft. x 6 ft. = 36 ft.^{2}

4.

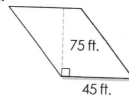

75 ft.

45 ft.

5.

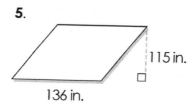

115 in.

136 in.

6.

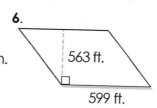

563 ft.

599 ft.

Lesson 5

Finding Area of Trapezoids

To find the **area** of a **trapezoid** use this formula:

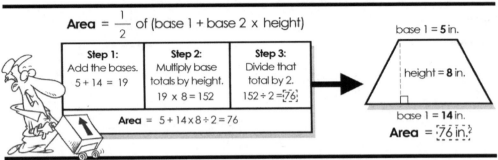

$$Area = \frac{1}{2} \text{ of (base 1 + base 2 x height)}$$

Step 1: Add the bases. 5 + 14 = 19	Step 2: Multiply base totals by height. 19 x 8 = 152	Step 3: Divide that total by 2. 152 ÷ 2 = 76

Area = 5 + 14 x 8 ÷ 2 = 76

base 1 = **5** in.

height = **8** in.

base 1 = **14** in.

Area = 76 in.²

Find the area of each trapezoid. Write the problem out.

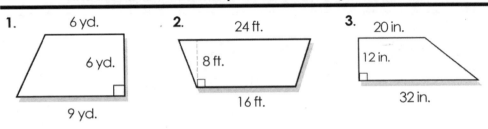

1.   6 yd.

6 yd.

9 yd.

6 + 9 x 6 ÷ 2 = 45 yd.²

2.   24 ft.

8 ft.

16 ft.

_____

3.   20 in.

12 in.

32 in.

_____

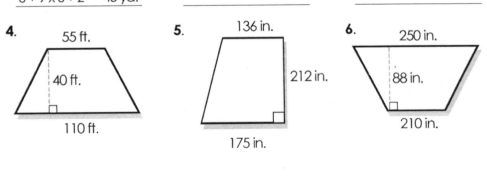

4.   55 ft.

40 ft.

110 ft.

_____

5.   136 in.

212 in.

175 in.

_____

6.   250 in.

88 in.

210 in.

_____

Lesson 6

Finding Perimeter 1

Perimeter is the distance around an object.
Find the perimeter of each object by adding all the sides.

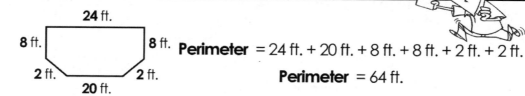

Perimeter = 24 ft. + 20 ft. + 8 ft. + 8 ft. + 2 ft. + 2 ft.

Perimeter = 64 ft.

Find the perimeter of each shape. Write the problem out.

1.   55 yd.

36 yd.   42 yd.

67 yd.

36 + 67 + 55 + 42 = 197 yd.

2.   125 ft.   89 ft.

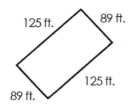

89 ft.   125 ft.

_____

3.   123 in.   324 in.

215 in.

107 in.

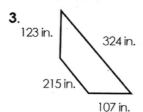

_____

4.   75 ft.

347 ft.   101 ft.

289 ft.

62 ft.

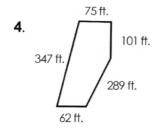

5.   572 in.   468 in.

635 in.

_____

6.   917 yd.

234 yd.   705 yd.

917 yd.

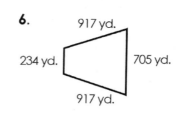

_____

Finding Perimeter 2

Find the perimeter of each shape. Write the problem out.

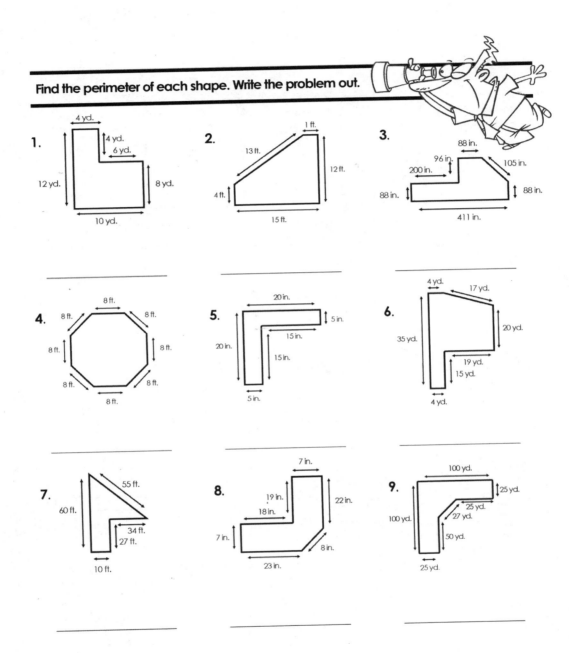

1. 4 yd. / 4 yd. / 6 yd. / 12 yd. / 8 yd. / 10 yd.

2. 1 ft. / 13 ft. / 12 ft. / 4 ft. / 15 ft.

3. 88 in. / 96 in. / 105 in. / 200 in. / 88 in. / 88 in. / 411 in.

4. 8 ft. / 8 ft. / 8 ft. / 8 ft. / 8 ft. / 8 ft. / 8 ft. / 8 ft.

5. 20 in. / 5 in. / 15 in. / 20 in. / 15 in. / 5 in.

6. 4 yd. / 17 yd. / 20 yd. / 35 yd. / 19 yd. / 15 yd. / 4 yd.

7. 55 ft. / 60 ft. / 34 ft. / 27 ft. / 10 ft.

8. 7 in. / 19 in. / 22 in. / 18 in. / 7 in. / 8 in. / 23 in.

9. 100 yd. / 25 yd. / 25 yd. / 27 yd. / 100 yd. / 50 yd. / 25 yd.

Lesson 7

Identifying Points, Lines and Rays

A **point** is an exact location in space.	A **line** is an endless straight path.	A **line segment** is a straight path between two points.	A **ray** is a part of a line; it has one endpoint and continues on in one direction.	A **vertex** is a point where two or more rays or line segments meet or cross.

Identify and write how many of each set of figures below.

1.

vertex, 1

ray, 2

point, 2

2.

3.

4.

5.

6.

7.

8.

Lesson 8

Identifying Parts of an Angle

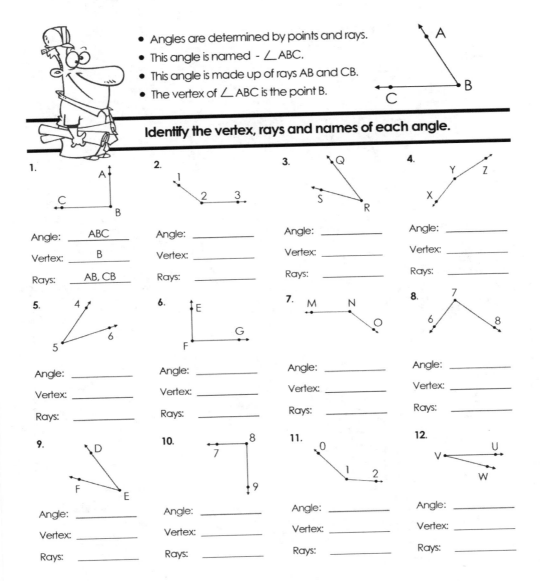

- Angles are determined by points and rays.
- This angle is named - ∠ ABC.
- This angle is made up of rays AB and CB.
- The vertex of ∠ ABC is the point B.

Identify the vertex, rays and names of each angle.

1.

Angle: _____ABC_____

Vertex: _____B_____

Rays: _____AB, CB_____

2.

Angle: _____

Vertex: _____

Rays: _____

3.

Angle: _____

Vertex: _____

Rays: _____

4.

Angle: _____

Vertex: _____

Rays: _____

5.

Angle: _____

Vertex: _____

Rays: _____

6.

Angle: _____

Vertex: _____

Rays: _____

7.

Angle: _____

Vertex: _____

Rays: _____

8.

Angle: _____

Vertex: _____

Rays: _____

9.

Angle: _____

Vertex: _____

Rays: _____

10.

Angle: _____

Vertex: _____

Rays: _____

11.

Angle: _____

Vertex: _____

Rays: _____

12.

Angle: _____

Vertex: _____

Rays: _____

Solid Shapes

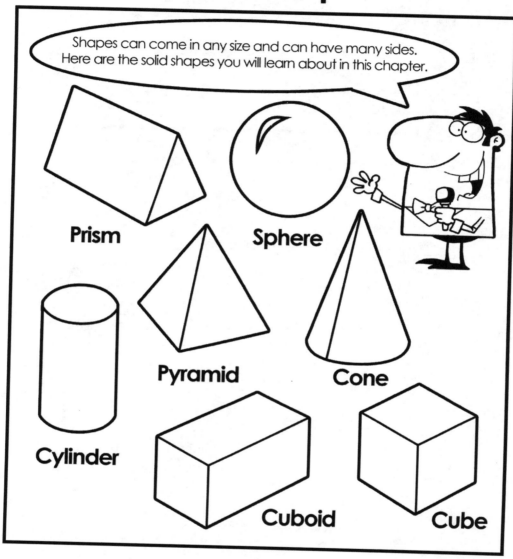

Shapes can come in any size and can have many sides. Here are the solid shapes you will learn about in this chapter.

Prism

Sphere

Pyramid

Cone

Cylinder

Cuboid

Cube

Lesson 9

Identifying Solid Shapes 1

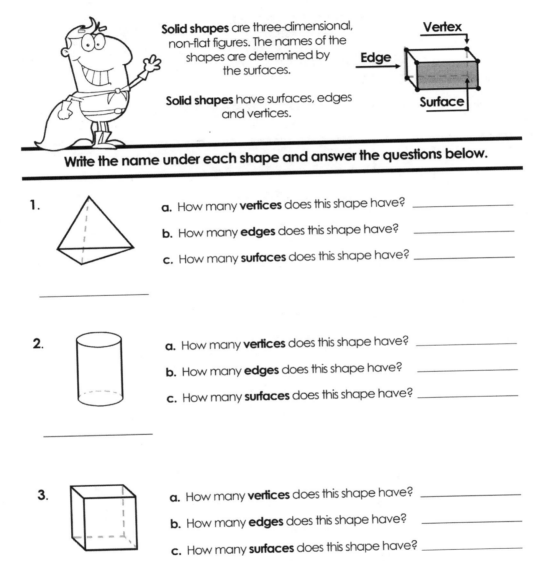

Solid shapes are three-dimensional, non-flat figures. The names of the shapes are determined by the surfaces.

Solid shapes have surfaces, edges and vertices.

Vertex

Edge

Surface

Write the name under each shape and answer the questions below.

1.

   a. How many **vertices** does this shape have? _____

   b. How many **edges** does this shape have? _____

   c. How many **surfaces** does this shape have? _____

_____

2.

   a. How many **vertices** does this shape have? _____

   b. How many **edges** does this shape have? _____

   c. How many **surfaces** does this shape have? _____

_____

3.

   a. How many **vertices** does this shape have? _____

   b. How many **edges** does this shape have? _____

   c. How many **surfaces** does this shape have? _____

_____

Identifying Solid Shapes 2

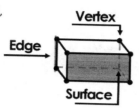

Solid shapes are three-dimensional, non-flat figures. The names of the shapes are determined by the surfaces.

Solid shapes have surfaces, edges and vertices.

Vertex

Edge

Surface

Write the name under each shape and answer the questions below.

1.

    a. How many **vertices** does this shape have? _____

    b. How many **edges** does this shape have? _____

    c. How many **surfaces** does this shape have? _____

_____

2.

    a. How many **vertices** does this shape have? _____

    b. How many **edges** does this shape have? _____

    c. How many **surfaces** does this shape have? _____

_____

3.

    a. How many **vertices** does this shape have? _____

    b. How many **edges** does this shape have? _____

    c. How many **surfaces** does this shape have? _____

_____

Lesson 10

Circles

Now we will learn about the components that make up a circle. With a circle we have the **radius**, **diameter** and the **circumference**. Knowing these components will help you to solve problems related to circles.

Radius

The **radius** of a circle is the distance from the circle's center point to any point on the circle. It can be used to determine a circle's diameter, circumference and area. Because of the circle's shape, the radius can be drawn in anywhere in the center of the circle.

Use this formula to find the radius of a circle:
Radius = Diameter ÷ 2

Diameter

The **diameter** of a circle is the length of a straight line through the center of a circle and touching two points on its edge, the diameter is twice the measurement of the radius. It is the longest distance across the circle. If the diameter of a circle is known, dividing it by two will equal the radius.

Use this formula to find the diameter of a circle:
Diameter = Radius x 2

Circumference

A circle's **circumference** is the distance around the circle. To determine the circumference of a circle, multiply the diameter by pi (π), or multiply the radius by 2 then multiply by pi (π). π is a Greek letter used in math to represent 3.14.

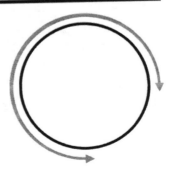

Use this formula to find the diameter of a circle:
Circumference = π x diameter or π x radius x 2

Lesson 11

Identifying Parts of a Circle

Identify the parts of the circles below.

1.

Circle: _____ A _____

Radius: _____ AB, AC, AD _____

Diameter: _____ BC _____

2.

Circle: _____

Radius: _____

Diameter: _____

3.

Circle: _____

Radius: _____

Diameter: _____

4.

Circle: _____

Radius: _____

Diameter: _____

5.

Circle: _____

Radius: _____

Diameter: _____

6.

Circle: _____

Radius: _____

Diameter: _____

Lesson 12

Finding the Radius of a Circle

The **radius** of a circle is the distance from the circle's center point to any point on the circle. It can be used to determine a circle's diameter, circumference and area. To find the radius divide the diameter by 2.

Radius = Diameter ÷ 2

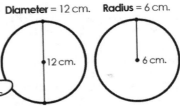

Diameter = 12 cm.   Radius = 6 cm.

Radius = 12 ÷ 2 = 6 cm.

Using the diameter, determine the radius of each circle.

1.

18 cm.

Radius: _18 ÷ 2 = 9 cm._

2.

36 in.

Radius: _____

3.

112 ft.

Radius: _____

4.

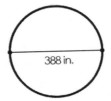

388 in.

Radius: _____

5.

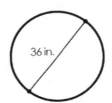

956 ft.

Radius: _____

6.

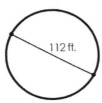

3,624 cm.

Radius: _____

- 125 -

Lesson 12

Finding the Diameter of a Circle

The **diameter** of a circle is defined as the length of a straight line through the center of a circle and touching two points on its edge, the diameter is twice the measurement of the radius. It is the longest distance across the circle. If the radius of a circle is known, multiplying it by two will equal the diameter.

Diameter = Radius x 2

Radius = 8 cm.   Diameter = 16 cm.

8 cm.   16 cm.

Diameter = 8 x 2 = 16cm.

Using the radius, determine the diameter of each circle.

1. 12 in.

2. 29 cm.

3. 89 ft.

Radius: ___12 x 2 = 24 in.___

Radius: _____

Radius: _____

4. 113 cm.

5. 624 in.

6. 2,935 ft.

Radius: _____

Radius: _____

Radius: _____

Lesson 13

Finding the Circumference of a Circle

A circle's **circumference** is the distance around the circle. To determine the circumference of a circle, multiply the diameter by pi (π), or multiply the radius by 2 then multiply by pi (π). π is a Greek letter used in mathematics to represent 3.14.

Radius = 4 cm.   **Diameter** = 8 cm.

4 cm.   8 cm.

Circumference   Circumference
4 × 3.14 × 2 = 25.12   8 × 3.14 = 25.12

Use these formulas to find the circumference of a circle:
Circumference = (π × diameter) or (π × radius × 2)
Circumference = (3.14 × diameter) or (3.14 × radius × 2)

Using the radius and diameter, determine the circumference of each circle below.

1.
55 in.

Circumference: __345.4 in.__

2.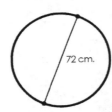
72 cm.

Circumference: _____

3.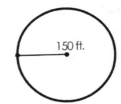
150 ft.

Circumference: _____

4.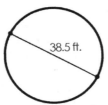
38.5 ft.

Circumference: _____

5.
531.4 in.

Circumference: _____

6.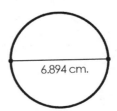
6.894 cm.

Circumference: _____

- 127 -

Chapter 7 - Graphs

In this chapter you will learn about the different types of graphs.

You will learn to read and create these types of graphs:

- Bar Graphs
- Line Graphs
- Pie Graphs

Graphs

A graph or chart is a diagram used to display data or information visually. There are three types of graphs: **Bar Graphs**, **Line Graphs** and **Pie Graphs**.

In this chapter you will learn to read and create these types of graphs.

A **bar graph** is useful for comparing facts and comparing quantities in different categories.

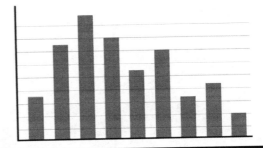

A **line graph** is used to display data or information that changes continuously over time.

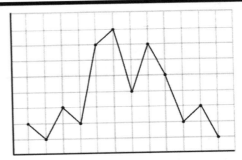

A **pie graph** or **circle graph** shows how the parts of something relate to the whole. It is divided into sectors, where each sector represents a particular category. The sections of this type of graph are usually represented by fractions.

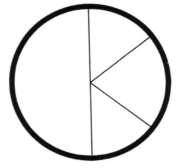

Lesson 1

Reading a Bar Graph 1

Our soccer team did well this year. Here is a graph of the points we scored each game.

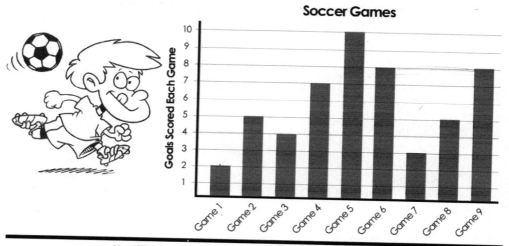

Use the bar graph to answer the questions below.

1. In which game did we score the highest number of goals? _____

2. In which game did we score the lowest number of goals? _____

3. How many goals did we score this entire season? _____

4. In game 9 we scored how many more goals than in game 3? _____

5. In game 5 we scored how many more goals than in game 7? _____

6. In games 2, 3 and 4 we scored how many goals in total? _____

7. In games 4, 5 and 6 we scored how many goals in total? _____

8. In which games did we score the same number of goals? _____

Reading a Bar Graph 2

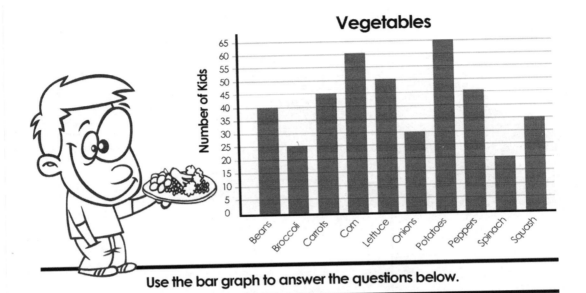

Vegetables

Use the bar graph to answer the questions below.

1. How many kids eat corn? _____

2. How many kids eat squash? _____

3. How many kids eat carrots? _____

4. How many kids eat onions? _____

5. How many kids eat peppers? _____

6. How many kids eat lettuce? _____

7. How many kids eat potatoes? _____

8. How many kids eat broccoli? _____

9. How many kids eat beans? _____

10. How many kids eat spinach? _____

11. How many kids prefer corn over squash? _____

12. How many kids prefer broccoli over spinach? _____

13. How many kids prefer potatoes over beans? _____

14. How many kids prefer lettuce over peppers? _____

15. How many kids prefer carrots over broccoli? _____

16. How many kids prefer corn over onions? _____

17. How many kids prefer potatoes over spinach? _____

18. How many kids prefer beans over onions? _____

Lesson 2

Creating a Bar Graph

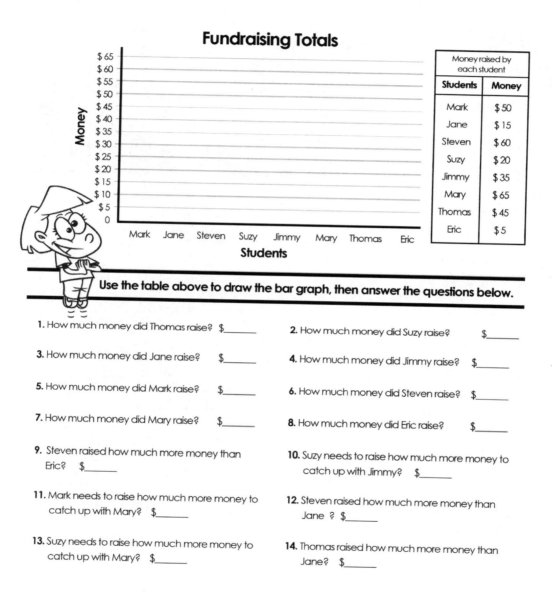

Fundraising Totals

Money raised by each student	
Students	**Money**
Mark	$ 50
Jane	$ 15
Steven	$ 60
Suzy	$ 20
Jimmy	$ 35
Mary	$ 65
Thomas	$ 45
Eric	$ 5

Use the table above to draw the bar graph, then answer the questions below.

1. How much money did Thomas raise? $_____

2. How much money did Suzy raise? $_____

3. How much money did Jane raise? $_____

4. How much money did Jimmy raise? $_____

5. How much money did Mark raise? $_____

6. How much money did Steven raise? $_____

7. How much money did Mary raise? $_____

8. How much money did Eric raise? $_____

9. Steven raised how much more money than Eric? $_____

10. Suzy needs to raise how much more money to catch up with Jimmy? $_____

11. Mark needs to raise how much more money to catch up with Mary? $_____

12. Steven raised how much more money than Jane ? $_____

13. Suzy needs to raise how much more money to catch up with Mary? $_____

14. Thomas raised how much more money than Jane? $_____

Lesson 3

Comparing Line Graphs

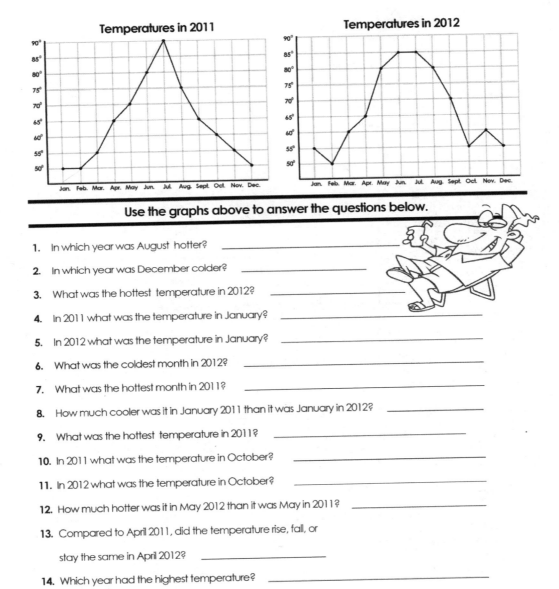

Use the graphs above to answer the questions below.

1. In which year was August hotter? _____

2. In which year was December colder? _____

3. What was the hottest temperature in 2012? _____

4. In 2011 what was the temperature in January? _____

5. In 2012 what was the temperature in January? _____

6. What was the coldest month in 2012? _____

7. What was the hottest month in 2011? _____

8. How much cooler was it in January 2011 than it was January in 2012? _____

9. What was the hottest temperature in 2011? _____

10. In 2011 what was the temperature in October? _____

11. In 2012 what was the temperature in October? _____

12. How much hotter was it in May 2012 than it was May in 2011? _____

13. Compared to April 2011, did the temperature rise, fall, or stay the same in April 2012? _____

14. Which year had the highest temperature? _____

- 133 -

Lesson 4

Creating a Line Graph

Line graphs use points and lines to show data visually.

Use the data on the left to draw your own line graph.
First plot the points, then draw a line connecting the points

Numbers of People in Museum	
Time	**People**
9 am	20
10 am	55
11 am	30
12 pm	10
1 pm	45
2 pm	65
3 pm	60
4 pm	40
5 pm	55
6 pm	15

Museum Attendance

Use the line graph you just drew to answer the questions below.

1. At what time was the attendance in the museum the highest? _____

2. At what time was the attendance in the museum the lowest? _____

3. How many people were in the museum at noon? _____

4. How many people were in the museum at 9am? _____

5. How many people were in the museum at 4pm? _____

6. How many more people were the in the museum at 5pm compared to 11am? _____

7. From 1pm to 2pm, how many people showed up at the museum? _____

8. From 5pm to 6pm, how many people left the museum? _____

9. During what one-hour time period did the attendance increase the most? _____

10. During what one-hour time period did the attendance decrease the most? _____

Lesson 5

Identifying Points on a Graph

Graphs are used to show information in a visual form.

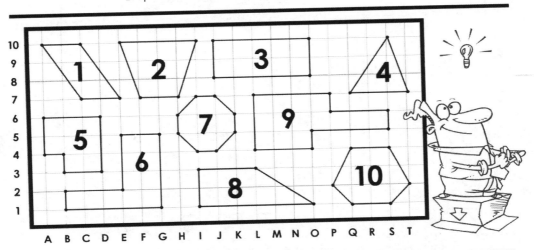

Using the graph above, write out the points that make up each shape.

1. A10, C10, C7, E7

2. _____

3. _____

4. _____

5. _____

6. _____

7. _____

8. _____

9. _____

10. _____

Lesson 6

Plotting Points on a Graph

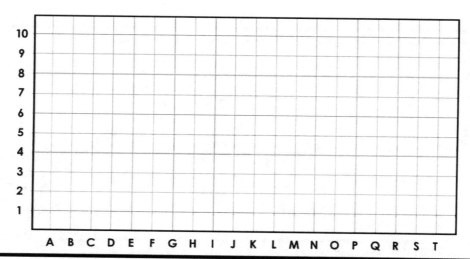

Using the coordinates below, plot the points on the graph above.
Draw a line between the points on the graph to create geometric shapes
and the write the name for each shape in the blanks.

1. A4, B1, E1, F4   trapezoid

2. G3, i3, G1, i1   _____

3. H6, L6, H4, L4   _____

4. P7, R10, T7   _____

5. F7, i10, L10, i7   _____

6. N8, M5, N2, O5   _____

7. P4, R5, T4, Q1, S1   _____

Lesson 7

Reading a Pie Chart 1

A **pie graph** shows how the parts of something relate to the whole.
It is divided into sectors. Each sector represents a particular category.

Use the graphs below to answer the questions.

Students' Favorite Classes

Kids' Favorite Pets

1. Which class do the students like most?

   _____

2. Which class do the students like the least?

   _____

3. What is the second-favorite class?

   _____

4. Which class do the students like more, math or reading?

   _____

5. What is the kids' favorite pet?

   _____

6. What is the kids' least favorite pet?

   _____

7. What is the kids' second favorite pet?

   _____

8. Do more kids' want a gerbil or fish?

   _____

Lesson 8

Reading a Pie Chart 2a

Shoe types that family members prefer.

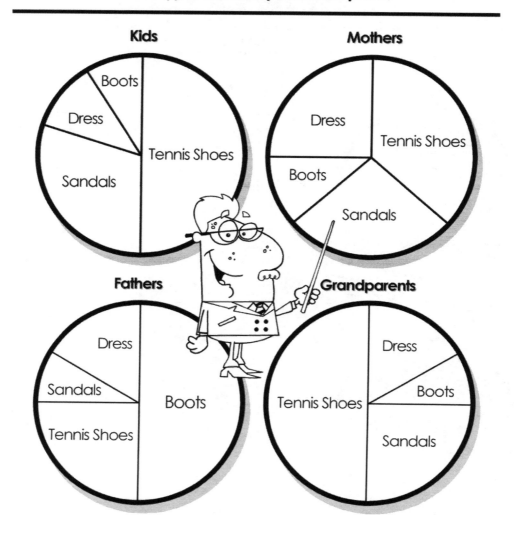

Lesson 9

Reading a Pie Chart 2b

Use the pie charts on the last page to answer the questions below.

1. Which shoes do kids like the most? _____

2. Which shoes do grandparents like the most? _____

3. Which shoes do mothers like the most? _____

4. Which shoes do fathers like the most? _____

5. What is the kids' second favorite shoes? _____

6. What is the fathers' second favorite shoes? _____

7. Which shoes do kids like least? _____

8. Which shoes do grandparents like least? _____

9. Which shoes do mothers like least? _____

10. Which shoes do fathers like least? _____

Lesson 10

Creating a Pie Chart

 A **pie graph** shows how the parts of something relate to the whole. It is divided into sectors. Each sector represents a particular category. The sum of all the parts will always equal 100%.

Using the information below, fill in the pie graphs with the correct numbers.

Most Studied Planets

1. Mars - 50%

2. Mercury - 6%

3. Venus - 10%

4. Neptune - 34%

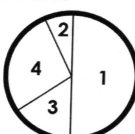

How Students Get to School

1. School Bus - 42%

2. Car - 35%

3. Bike - 15%

4. Walk - 8%

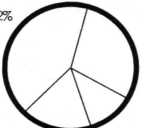

Favorite Movie Types in Schools

1. Comedy - 35%

2. Action - 18%

3. Drama - 8%

4. Animation - 24%

5. Science Fiction- 15%

Fish Population in the Pond

1. Bass - 20%

2. Catfish - 27%

3. Trout - 14%

4. Guppies - 32%

5. Turtles - 7%

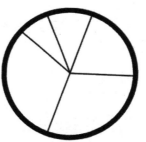

Practice Test #1

Practice Questions

1. What is the value of the digit 5 in the number 3,456,789?

Ⓐ Fifty thousand

Ⓑ Five thousand

Ⓒ Five-hundred thousand

Ⓓ Five million

2. In ice hockey, the number of points a player scores is defined as the sum of the number of goals and the number of assists. Which hockey player listed in the table below has the highest number of points?

Player	Goals	Assists
Phillips	2	23
Jackson	5	17
Robinson	13	15
Miller	8	19

Ⓐ Phillips

Ⓑ Jackson

Ⓒ Robinson

Ⓓ Miller

3. A recipe calls for $3\frac{3}{4}$ cups of flour. Which fraction below is equivalent to this amount?

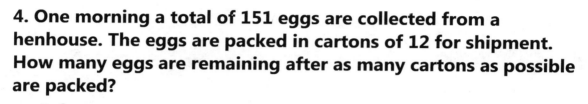

Ⓐ $\frac{5}{2}$

Ⓑ $\frac{15}{4}$

Ⓒ $\frac{3}{2}$

Ⓓ $\frac{9}{4}$

4. One morning a total of 151 eggs are collected from a henhouse. The eggs are packed in cartons of 12 for shipment. How many eggs are remaining after as many cartons as possible are packed?

Ⓐ 3

Ⓑ 9

Ⓒ 7

Ⓓ 1

5. Which numeral is in the thousandths place in 0.3874?

Ⓐ 3

Ⓑ 8

Ⓒ 7

Ⓓ 4

6. A rectangular plot in a garden is three times longer than it is wide. What is the perimeter of the garden if it has a width of 8 meters?

Ⓐ 32 meters

Ⓑ 192 meters

Ⓒ 24 meters

Ⓓ 64 meters

7. Part A: The number of customers in a new restaurant is given in the table below:

Week	Customers
1	155
2	180
3	205

How many customers should be expected in week 4?

Ⓐ 225

Ⓑ 230

Ⓒ 200

Ⓓ 255

Part B: The average meal at the restaurant is $12. How much money will they make in week 4?

_____

8. The rectangular prism below has a volume of 144 cu. cm. The length and width are given below. What is the height of the rectangular prism?

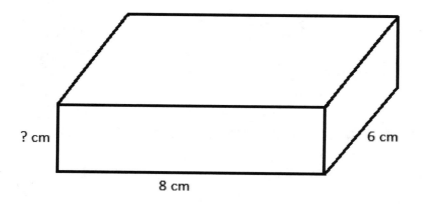

9. 0.58 - 0.39=

ⓐ 0.19

ⓑ 1.9

ⓒ 0.29

ⓓ 2.9

10. The recipe Mary is using to bake cupcakes requires 1 cup of milk and makes 8 cupcakes. If she needs to make 32 cupcakes for the party, how much milk is needed?

ⓐ 1 pint

ⓑ 1 gallon

ⓒ 3 cups

ⓓ 1 quart

11. Solve the equation: $\frac{2}{5} + \frac{3}{4} - \frac{1}{2} = ?$

_____

12. Which of the following is correct?

Ⓐ $\frac{4}{7} = \frac{12}{21}$

Ⓑ $\frac{3}{4} = \frac{12}{20}$

Ⓒ $\frac{5}{8} = \frac{15}{32}$

Ⓓ $\frac{7}{9} = \frac{28}{35}$

13. Donnie has a baseball card that is 4.2 inches tall and 2.6 inches wide. What is the area of the card?

_____

14. An electronics store sells _E_ Evercell brand batteries in packages of 4 and _D_ Durapower brand batteries in packages of 6. Which expression represents the total number of batteries in the store?

Ⓐ $(4 + E) \times (6 + D)$

Ⓑ $(4 \times E) + (6 \times D)$

Ⓒ $(4 + E) + (6 + D)$

Ⓓ $(4 \times E) \div (6 \times D)$

15. At the park there is a walking trail that goes around the perimeter. One lap around the park is .28 miles. Samantha walks 11 laps. How far has she walked?

_____

16. Solve the equations below:

$.3 \times 1.25 =?$

$1.22 - .85 + .34 =?$

$(.22 + 1.48) \times .5 =?$

17. Given the figure of the parallelogram below, which side is parallel to side $\overline{RT}$?

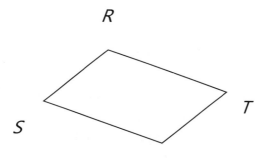

Ⓐ $\overline{RS}$

Ⓑ $\overline{QS}$

Ⓒ $\overline{QT}$

Ⓓ None of the above

18. A fish tank is a rectangular prism with a length of 7 inches and a width of 5 inches and can hold a volume of 210 cubic inches of water. What is the height of the tank?

Ⓐ 6 inches

Ⓑ 5 inches

Ⓒ 17.5 inches

Ⓓ 10 inches

19. The all-time rushing leader in professional football ran for 18,335 yards in his career. What is the best whole number approximation of the number of miles he ran?

_____

20. A survey of a random sample of 100 drivers asked them the color of their car. The results of the survey are presented in the table below.

Color of car	Number of drivers
Blue	26
Red	14
Yellow	36
Silver	24

If the parking lot at the local store is filled with 25 cars, how many yellow cars would be expected to be in the lot?

Ⓐ 6

Ⓑ 9

Ⓒ 11

Ⓓ 12

21. Cindy earned $100 one week at the ice cream stand. She put $\frac{1}{4}$ of the money in her savings account and kept the rest as cash. After this, she received a cash bonus of $20 from the owner of the ice cream stand and didn't put any of it in the savings account. Which expression represents the amount of cash Cindy currently has?

Ⓐ $C = \frac{3}{4}(100) + 20$

Ⓑ $C = \frac{1}{4}(100) + 20$

Ⓒ $C = \frac{1}{4}(100) - 20$

Ⓓ $C = \frac{3}{4}(120)$

22. Mr. Thompson fills his 25.2 gallon gasoline tank with gas that costs $2.98 a gallon. Which is the best approximation of the cost of the gasoline?

Ⓐ $50

Ⓑ $60

Ⓒ $75

Ⓓ $90

23. Using the order of operations solve the problem below.

$8 \times (5 - 2) + (4 + 5) =$ _____

24. Janice gets home from school at 2:45 PM. She does homework for 1 hour and 30 minutes, then goes out and plays for 1 hour and 45 minutes before returning home for dinner. What time is it when Janice returns home for dinner?

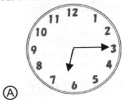

Ⓐ

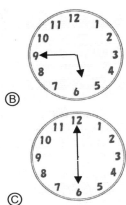

Ⓑ

Ⓒ

Ⓓ

25. Two sisters were arguing who could have a larger piece of pie. Their mother told the older daughter she could have 2/5 of the pie. She told the younger daughter she could have 1/3 of the pie. Which daughter received a larger piece of pie?

Ⓐ The older daughter.

Ⓑ The younger daughter

Ⓒ Same size piece for each daughter

Ⓓ Not enough information to determine

26. It takes Jack 14.67 minutes to get to school in the morning. It only takes Clayton 10.24 minutes to get to school. How much less time does it take Jack to get to school?

_____

27. A ship is located on the map at coordinates (4, 9). If the radar indicates the lighthouse is 5 units east and 4 units south of the ship, what is the location of the lighthouse?

Ⓐ (9, 5)

Ⓑ (9, 4)

Ⓒ (8.

Nort

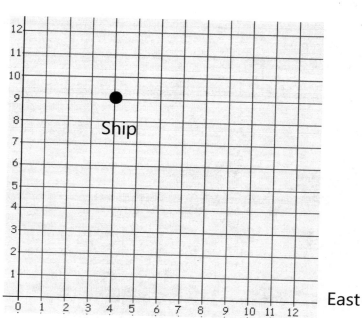

East

28. When taking a person's temperature with an oral thermometer, temperatures between 96.9° and 99.5° are considered normal. Which temperature below is outside of the normal range?

Ⓐ 97.2°

Ⓑ 99.3°

Ⓒ 98.9°

Ⓓ 96.3°

29. The high temperatures in degrees Celsius for a work week are given on the table below:

Day	Monday	Tuesday	Wednesday	Thursday	Friday
High Temp.	9	16	13	20	22

What was the mean high temperature for the week?

Ⓐ 14

Ⓑ 16

Ⓒ 13

Ⓓ 22

30. On the graph below plot the points (6,9), (3,8), and (-2,4).

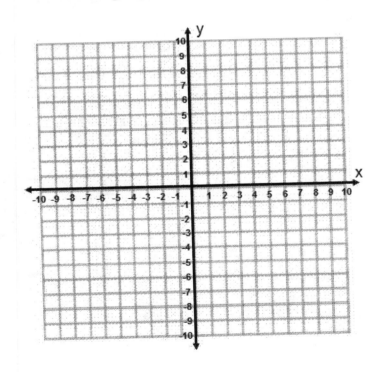

31. A little league has 92 children sign up for baseball season. If each team needs at least 14 players, how many complete baseball teams can be formed?

Ⓐ 5

Ⓑ 6

Ⓒ 7

Ⓓ 8

32. Part A: Given the isosceles trapezoid PQRS below, which two sides are congruent?

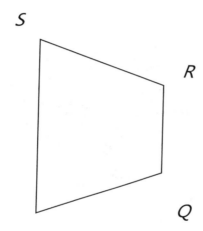

Ⓐ $\overline{PS}$ and $\overline{QR}$

Ⓑ $\overline{RS}$ and $\overline{QF}$ P

Ⓒ $\overline{QP}$ and $\overline{RQ}$

Ⓓ $\overline{PS}$ and $\overline{RS}$

Part B: Which two sides are parallel?

Ⓐ $\overline{PS}$ and $\overline{QR}$

Ⓑ $\overline{RS}$ and $\overline{QF}$ P

Ⓒ $\overline{QP}$ and $\overline{RQ}$

Ⓓ $\overline{PS}$ and $\overline{RS}$

33. A length of string is measured to be $\frac{31}{8}$ inches. Between which two points on the ruler below will this length lie?

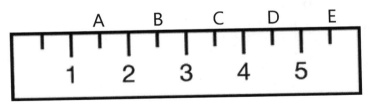

Ⓐ Between points A and B

Ⓑ Between points B and C

Ⓒ Between points C and D

Ⓓ Between points D and E

34. Which point lies within the shaded region below?

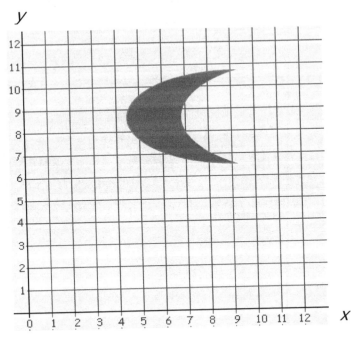

Ⓐ (5, 6)

Ⓑ (8, 6)

Ⓒ (7, 10)

Ⓓ (9, 9)

35. The model shown below represents $1\frac{7}{10}$

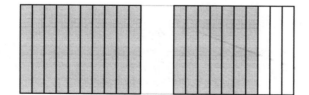

Which decimal does this also represent?

Ⓐ 0.7

Ⓑ 0.07

Ⓒ 1.7

Ⓓ 1.07

36. An electronics store sells T.V.'s for $525 and game systems for $250. If 36 people buy T.V. and 29 people buy a game system how much money would the store make?

---

37. Of the 20 people in Joan's class, 4 of them have birthdays in the winter, 7 have birthdays in the spring, 3 have birthdays in the summer, and 6 have birthdays in the fall. What is the probability a student chosen at random will have a birthday in either the spring or the summer?

Ⓐ $\frac{7}{20}$

Ⓑ $\frac{1}{2}$

Ⓒ $\frac{3}{20}$

Ⓓ $\frac{3}{10}$

38. Phil is going to school overseas for 9 weeks and 5 days. How many days will Phil be gone?

    Ⓐ 95

    Ⓑ 44

    Ⓒ 59

    Ⓓ 68

39. Julie shopped for first-aid cream. One large tube held 1.5 fluid ounces and the smallest tube held 0.33 fluid ounces. What is the difference in the number of fluid ounces of cream in the two tubes?

    Ⓐ 1.8

    Ⓑ 1.27

    Ⓒ 1.23

    Ⓓ 1.17

40. Jan played a game which used a fair spinner like the one shown here. Jan needs the arrow to land on green on her next turn.

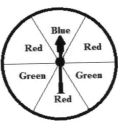

What is the probability that the arrow lands on green when Jan spins one time?

    Ⓐ $\frac{1}{6}$

    Ⓑ $\frac{1}{3}$

    Ⓒ $\frac{1}{2}$

    Ⓓ $\frac{2}{3}$

Practice Test #2

Practice Questions

1. Which number represents "fifty-seven thousand three hundred and forty"?

Ⓐ 570,340

Ⓑ 573,400

Ⓒ 5,734

Ⓓ 57,340

2. Four students were given a typing test measuring their speed in words per minute and then given the same typing test several weeks later. Which student had the greatest improvement?

Student	First score (words per minute)	Second score (words per minute)
Alexander	22	39
Betty	39	48
Carolyn	27	43
David	22	42

Ⓐ Alexander

Ⓑ Betty

Ⓒ Carolyn

Ⓓ David

3. A bookshelf is to be $7\frac{5}{8}$ inches wide. Which fraction below is equivalent to this measurement?

Ⓐ $\frac{35}{8}$

Ⓑ $\frac{75}{8}$

Ⓒ $\frac{61}{8}$

Ⓓ $\frac{43}{8}$

4. Toasty Donut Shop makes 141 donuts one morning. The donuts are packaged in boxes of 12 for delivery. How many single donuts are left over?

Ⓐ 3

Ⓑ 9

Ⓒ 6

Ⓓ 1

5. Which numeral is in the thousandths place in .5643?

Ⓐ 5

Ⓑ 6

Ⓒ 4

Ⓓ 3

6. Dennis weighs 56 pounds. His little brother Donny weighs 23 pounds less than him. What is Donny's weight in ounces?

_____

7. A square flower garden has an area of 81 feet. What is the length of one side of the garden?

Ⓐ 9 feet

Ⓑ 20.25 feet

Ⓒ 40.5 feet

Ⓓ 324 feet

8. Which of the following is correct?

Ⓐ $\dfrac{2}{3} = \dfrac{18}{24}$

Ⓑ $\dfrac{4}{5} = \dfrac{16}{20}$

Ⓒ $\dfrac{1}{9} = \dfrac{4}{18}$

Ⓓ $\dfrac{3}{8} = \dfrac{9}{16}$

9. Round each of the decimals below to the nearest hundredth.

$3.116 \approx$ _____

$3.081 \approx$ _____

$3.006 \approx$ _____

$3.107 \approx$ _____

10. Which of the following figures is a trapezoid?

Ⓐ

Ⓑ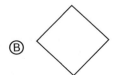

Ⓒ

Ⓓ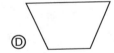

11. A gallon of cooking oil is used to make popcorn for 256 people. How much cooking oil is needed to make popcorn for 96 people?

Ⓐ 2 quarts

Ⓑ 3 pints

Ⓒ 1 quart

Ⓓ 1 cup

12. Jodi made a sum of money yesterday at a bake sale. She spent half of the money to buy more ingredients for next week's bake sale, and then spent $12 to go to the movies. Jodi has $17 remaining. How much did she make yesterday at the bake sale?

Ⓐ $36

Ⓑ $58

Ⓒ $46

Ⓓ $41

13. Express 99/14 as a mixed fraction.

Ⓐ $7\frac{1}{14}$

Ⓑ $7\frac{3}{14}$

Ⓒ $7\frac{11}{14}$

Ⓓ $7\frac{5}{14}$

14. A little boy decides to give away all of his marbles. Each of his 4 friends is to receive an equal share. Which of the statements below describes how this can be done?

    Ⓐ Multiply his marbles by 4 and give this amount to each of his friends

    Ⓑ Multiply his marbles by 2 and give this amount to each of his friends

    Ⓒ Multiply his marbles by 1/2 and give this amount to each of his friends

    Ⓓ Multiply his marbles by 1/4 and give this amount to each of his friends

15. Part A: A store receives regular shipments of paper towels. Each shipment contains 26 boxes. Each box contains 6 packages and each package has 8 rolls of paper towels. How many rolls of paper towels come in one shipment?

_____

Part B: If the store sells 6100 rolls each month how many shipments will it need in one month?

_____

16. Part A: A zoo has three different lion enclosures. The first one is $\frac{5}{8}$ of an acre. The second one is $\frac{5}{6}$ of an acre. How much bigger is the second on than the first one?

_____

Part B: If the third one is $\frac{7}{12}$, what is the total number of acres in all three enclosures?

_____

17. Given the figure of the parallelogram below, which side is congruent to side $\overline{RT}$?

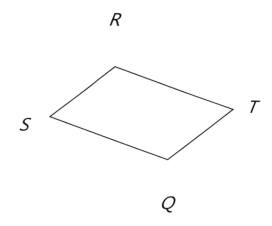

Ⓐ $\overline{RS}$

Ⓑ $\overline{QS}$

Ⓒ $\overline{QT}$

Ⓓ None of the above

18. A large rectangular-prism-shaped tank at the zoo is 8 feet wide and 5 feet high. How long is the tank if it holds a volume of 200 cubic feet of water?

   Ⓐ 8 feet

   Ⓑ 6 feet

   Ⓒ 13 feet

   Ⓓ 5 feet

19. Mount McKinley, the tallest mountain in North America, is 20,320 feet high. Approximately how many miles tall is the Mount?

   Ⓐ 6

   Ⓑ 5

   Ⓒ 4

   Ⓓ 3

20. Mrs. Jackson records the hair color of the 20 children in her room and obtains the following results:

Hair color	Number of students
Black	6
Brown	8
Blonde	4
Red	2

If the school has a total of 240 children, how many children with brown hair should be expected?

21. A grocery store determines the price of a gallon milk, _P_, in dollars will be determined by multiplying the wholesale price, _W_, in dollars by 1.5 and adding 25 cents. Which expression below represents this relationship?

Ⓐ $P = 1.5 + W + 0.25$

Ⓑ $P = 0.25W + 1.5$

Ⓒ $P = 1.75W$

Ⓓ $P = 1.5W + 0.25$

22. The movie Laura went to see ended at 8:15 PM. The movie she saw was 2 hours and 45 minutes long. What time did the movie start?

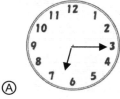
Ⓐ

Ⓑ

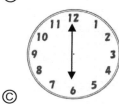
Ⓒ

Ⓓ

23. Using order of operations solve the problem below.

$3 + (9 - 4) \times (4 + 5) = ?$

_____

24. On Saturday Allen spent 73 minutes mowing the grass. He spent 42 minutes washing his car, another 56 minutes repairing a fence, and 31 minutes trimming the shrubs. How much time did he spend doing chores on Saturday?

Ⓐ 2 hours 51 minutes

Ⓑ 3 hours 22 minutes

Ⓒ 3 hours 18 minutes

Ⓓ 3 hours 28 minutes

25. Which one of the statements about the rectangular prism below is FALSE?

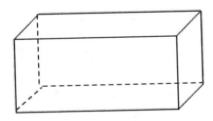

Ⓐ There are 12 edges on the rectangular prism.

Ⓑ The six sides of the rectangular prism all have the same area.

Ⓒ Some of the edges are parallel.

Ⓓ There are 8 vertices on the rectangular prism.

26. The model shown below represents $1\frac{5}{10}$

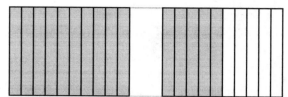

Which decimal does this also represent?

Ⓐ 0.5

Ⓑ 1.5

Ⓒ 1.05

Ⓓ 1.005

27. An observation tower is located at point (8, 5) on the map grid below. A fire is observed from a location 4 units west and 2 units north of the tower. What is the location of the fire?

Ⓐ (12, 7)

Ⓑ (4, 7)

Ⓒ (6, 9)

Ⓓ (4, 5)

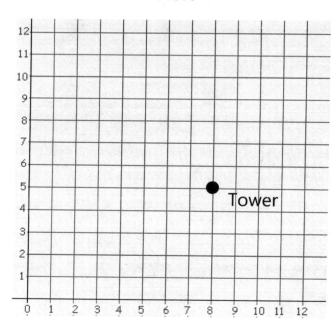

28. Maria is moving and needs a box to pack books in. The box needs to be 416 cubic inches. Which of the following boxes is the right size?

Ⓐ a box that is $8\ in. \times 12\ in. \times 5\ in.$

Ⓑ a box that is $12\ in. \times 4\ in. \times 9\ in.$

Ⓒ a box that is $13\ in. \times 5\ in. \times 7\ in.$

Ⓓ a box that is $13\ in. \times 4\ in. \times 8\ in.$

29. The number of washes the Squeaky Clean car wash made last week is given in the table below:

Day	Monday	Tuesday	Wednesday	Thursday	Friday
Car Washes	22	28	38	47	45

What is the mean number of car washes for the week?

Ⓐ 44

Ⓑ 47

Ⓒ 36

Ⓓ 31

30. 0.28 x 0.17

Ⓐ 0.2260

Ⓑ 0.4760

Ⓒ 0.0226

Ⓓ 0.0476

31. Jim brings two ice chests to the beach. Ice chest A has two compartments, while Ice Chest B just has one. Ice chest B can hold 24 drinks while Ice chest A can hold twice as many. If the larger compartment in Ice Chest A holds 34, how many does the smaller one hold?

_____

32. Mandy's Farmer's Market sells pears in boxes of 18. A shipment of 417 pears arrives that morning. How many full boxes of pears can Mandy sell using that shipment?

Ⓐ 25

Ⓑ 23

Ⓒ 18

Ⓓ 20

33. The side length of a regular pentagon is 6.5 centimeters. What is the perimeter of this figure?

Ⓐ 26.0 cm.

Ⓑ 42.25 cm.

Ⓒ 39.0 cm.

Ⓓ 32.5 cm.

34. A length of yarn is measured to be $\frac{35}{8}$ inches. Between which points on the ruler will this length lie?

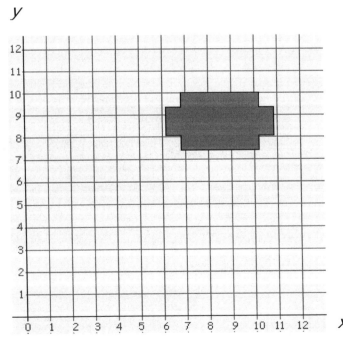

Ⓐ Between points A and B

Ⓑ Between points B and C

Ⓒ Between points C and D

Ⓓ Between points D and E

35

25. Which point lies within the shaded region below?

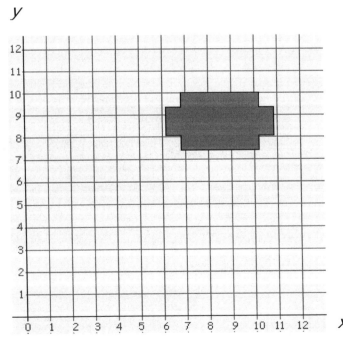

Ⓐ (5, 8)

Ⓑ (8, 9)

Ⓒ (7, 11)

Ⓓ (9, 7)

36 **26. The workers at a large construction site were made up of 11 plumbers, 7 electricians, 13 carpenters, 8 concrete finishers and 11 laborers. What is the probability that a worker chosen at random will be either a carpenter or an electrician?**

Ⓐ $\frac{13}{50}$

Ⓑ $\frac{9}{25}$

Ⓒ $\frac{2}{5}$

Ⓓ $\frac{7}{25}$

27. Which line graph correctly reflects the data shown in the table?

Time	Number of Customers
2:00 pm	20
4:00 pm	30
6:00 pm	50
8:00 pm	10

Ⓐ

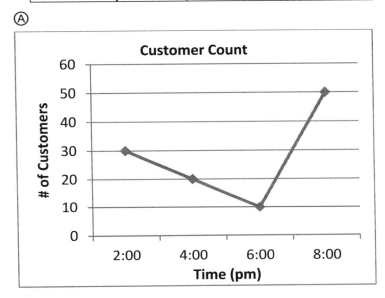

Ⓑ

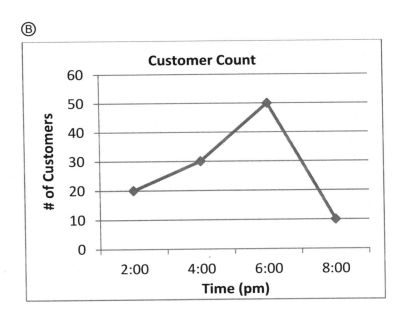

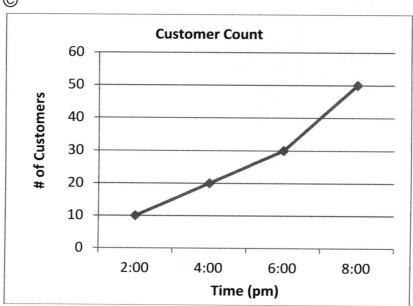

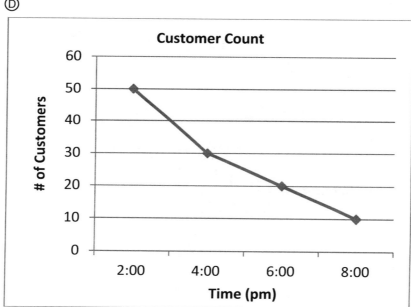

28. Four students measured the length of the pencil each was using. The list shows the lengths, in centimeters, of the four pencils.

17.03 cm, 17.4 cm, 17.31 cm, 17.09 cm

Which list shows the lengths of the pencils in order, from shortest to longest?

Ⓐ *17.4 cm, 17.31 cm, 17.09 cm, 17.03 cm*

Ⓑ *17.03 cm, 17.09 cm, 17.4 cm, 17.31 cm*

Ⓒ *17.4 cm, 17.03 cm, 17.09 cm, 17.31 cm*

Ⓓ *17.03 cm, 17.09 cm, 17.31 cm, 17.4 cm*

29. What is the equivalent decimal number for five hundred twelve thousandths?

Ⓐ 0.512

Ⓑ 0.0512

Ⓒ 5120.

Ⓓ 0.00512

40. Reduce $\frac{14}{98}$ to lowest terms.

Ⓐ $\frac{7}{49}$

Ⓑ $\frac{2}{14}$

Ⓒ $\frac{1}{7}$

Ⓓ $\frac{3}{8}$

Thank You

We at Mometrix would like to extend our heartfelt thanks to you, our friend and patron, for allowing us to play a part in your journey. It is a privilege to serve people from all walks of life who are unified in their commitment to building the best future they can for themselves.

The preparation you devote to these important testing milestones may be the most valuable educational opportunity you have for making a real difference in your life. We encourage you to put your heart into it—that feeling of succeeding, overcoming, and yes, conquering will be well worth the hours you've invested.

We want to hear your story, your struggles and your successes, and if you see any opportunities for us to improve our materials so we can help others even more effectively in the future, please share that with us as well. **The team at Mometrix would be absolutely thrilled to hear from you!** So please, send us an email (support@mometrix.com) and let's stay in touch.

Additional Bonus Material

Due to our efforts to try to keep this book to a manageable length, we've created a link that will give you access to all of your additional bonus material.

Please visit http://www.mometrix.com/bonus948/fsag5mathwb to access the information.

TABLE OF CONTENTS

Workbook Answers

Chapter 1 - Whole Numbers

Pg 6

1.

Ten Millions	Millions	Hundred Thousands	Ten Thousands	Thousands	Hundreds	Tens	Ones
1	5	6	3	2	7	8	2

2.

Ten Millions	Millions	Hundred Thousands	Ten Thousands	Thousands	Hundreds	Tens	Ones
2	4	8	7	9	3	6	0

3.

Ten Millions	Millions	Hundred Thousands	Ten Thousands	Thousands	Hundreds	Tens	Ones
6	2	1	5	8	5	2	4

4.

Ten Millions	Millions	Hundred Thousands	Ten Thousands	Thousands	Hundreds	Tens	Ones
3	0	6	7	1	2	3	4

5.

Ten Millions	Millions	Hundred Thousands	Ten Thousands	Thousands	Hundreds	Tens	Ones
5	2	1	9	7	3	0	5

6.

Ten Millions	Millions	Hundred Thousands	Ten Thousands	Thousands	Hundreds	Tens	Ones
8	3	4	9	8	1	4	7

Pg 7

	Hundred Millions	Ten Millions	Millions	Hundred Thousands	Ten Thousands	Thousands	Hundreds	Tens	Ones
1.	7	4	8	4	2	2	7	1	9
2.	3	2	9	6	0	8	1	1	4
3.	1	2	4	3	7	5	2	7	7
4.	7	4	1	5	8	8	3	7	9
5.	5	0	4	2	6	7	3	3	2
6.	9	7	2	1	1	4	0	8	9

Pg 8		Pg 9		Pg 10	
No.	Answer	No.	Answer	No.	Answer
1	3,000	1	24,453	1	850 + 400 = 1,250
2	9,000	2	55,718	2	450 + 550 = 1,000
3	1,000	3	19,554	3	150 + 600 = 750
4	8,000	4	28,132	4	400 + 750 = 1,150
5	3,000	5	12,966	5	950 - 500 = 450
6	4,000	6	93,359	6	750 - 200 = 550
7	6,000	7	96,591	7	650 – 450 = 200
8	8,000	8	56,772	8	360 - 180 = 180
9	6,000	9	83,297		
10	2,000	10	27,915		
11	40,000	11	35,212		
12	20,000	12	62,689		
13	90,000	13	49,212		
14	60,000	14	79,359		
15	70,000	15	93,756		
16	80,000	16	41,328		
17	30,000	17	43,957		
18	40,000	18	14,161		
19	20,000	19	93,564		
20	50,000	20	39,817		
21	300,000				
22	600,000				
23	200,000				
24	500,000				
25	200,000				
26	300,000				
27	900,000				
28	600,000				
29	800,000				
30	100,000				

Pg 11		Pg 12		Pg 13	
No.	Answer	No.	Answer	No.	Answer
1	6,000 + 4,000 = 10,000	1	1,225	1	6,515
2	5,000 + 1,000 = 6,000	2	1,024	2	12,834
3	9,000 + 7,000 = 16,000	3	1,580	3	12,670
4	5,000 + 5,000 = 10,000	4	742	4	11,229
5	3,000 + 6,000 = 9,000	5	1,261	5	16,342
6	8,000 + 7,000 = 15,000	6	1,111	6	8,877
7	2,000 + 5,000 = 7,000	7	1,353	7	5,300
8	4,000 + 5,000 = 9,000	8	1,632	8	11,866
9	9,000 + 500 = 9,500	9	1,236	9	13,940
10	4,000 - 2,000 = 2,000	10	1,430	10	9,715
11	9,000 - 5,000 = 4,000			11	15,009
12	7,000 - 6,000 = 1,000			12	5,461
13	5,000 - 3,000 = 2,000			13	4,177
14	9,000 - 8,000 = 1,000			14	15,408
15	4,000 - 2,000 = 2,000			15	13,512
16	4,000 - 800 = 3,200			16	24,745
17	6,000 - 2,000 = 4,000			17	10,693
18	8,000 - 6,000 = 2,000			18	14,319
				19	14,792
				20	14,112

Pg 14		Pg 15		Pg 16	
No.	Answer	No.	Answer	No.	Answer
1	23,795	1	104,654	1	596,052
2	16,340	2	188,944	2	977,698
3	16,891	3	144,072	3	1,160,308
4	23,486	4	189,476	4	1,097,102
5	18,748	5	104,323	5	1,089,063
6	22,475	6	103,894	6	1,283,759
7	20,531	7	156,084	7	1,336,765
8	13,385	8	140,874	8	845,509
9	13,938	9	184,913	9	1,051,175
10	19,146	10	147,781	10	1,085,891
11	17,264	11	57,012	11	1,975,054
12	17,039	12	183,425	12	841,668
13	16,951	13	131,969	13	1,410,112
14	14,558	14	101,039	14	1,518,639
15	22,189	15	184,161	15	2,240,839
16	14,766	16	115,576	16	720,411
17	21,953	17	83,250	17	1,776,777
18	13,765	18	68,871	18	1,577,184
19	8,331	19	174,540	19	1,304,447
20	18,795	20	264,261	20	1,662,926

Pg 17		Pg 18		Pg 19	
No.	Answer	No.	Answer	No.	Answer
1	12,052,629	1	443	1	1,112
2	7,888,122	2	452	2	1,111
3	17,265,467	3	143	3	3,781
4	21,709,039	4	284	4	2,779
5	14,622,984	5	539	5	1,756
6	11,129,457	6	118	6	6,487
7	19,771,741	7	861	7	7,511
8	17,143,156	8	451	8	2,264
9	10,170,485	9	252	9	524
10	14,603,355	10	129	10	5,685
11	23,268,932	11	291	11	327
12	13,589,274	12	450	12	2,047
13	15,296,451	13	288	13	4,635
14	17,280,455	14	457	14	2,059
15	12,562,642	15	432	15	5,475
16	15,576,391			16	2,889
17	15,540,467			17	1,454
18	15,214,301			18	916
19	22,688,631			19	2,755
20	20,429,648			20	2,747

Pg 20		Pg 21		Pg 22	
No.	Answer	No.	Answer	No.	Answer
1	2,786	1	131,482	1	592,288
2	25,038	2	507,851	2	1,409,294
3	21,376	3	277,758	3	5,730,630
4	36,508	4	34,013	4	2,437,389
5	20,756	5	778,375	5	2,113,834
6	16,804	6	191,436	6	5,220,339
7	20,507	7	411,246	7	7,314,169
8	4,557	8	352,113	8	2,876,907
9	37,509	9	221,963	9	3,135,552
10	38,809	10	232,179	10	5,127,660
11	18,499	11	47,078	11	1,801,944
12	26,055	12	181,244	12	4,683,052
13	15,864	13	426,781	13	3,125,607
14	43,464	14	151,044	14	4,587,627
15	45,132	15	374,747	15	3,670,658
16	46,172	16	96,861	16	3,371,113
17	18,489	17	189,668	17	6,478,871
18	21,529	18	412,017	18	2,359,169
19	57,435	19	199,681	19	3,467,162
20	76,939	20	619,306	20	2,282,335

Pg 23	
No.	Answer
1	13,138,506
2	30,680,207
3	22,547,298
4	35,657,655
5	7,593,206
6	46,473,155
7	55,559,777
8	89,277,747
9	34,798,707
10	19,262,091
11	86,135,587
12	29,474,647
13	64,926,012
14	43,864,964
15	30,236,771
16	37,778,627
17	81,291,709
18	37,006,688
19	56,327,553
20	38,185,370
21	66,798,298
22	75,126,679
23	15,285,265
24	32,454,367

Multiplication Table

x	1	2	3	4	5	6	7	8	9	10
1	1	2	3	4	5	6	7	8	9	10
2	2	4	6	8	10	12	14	16	18	20
3	3	6	9	12	15	18	21	24	27	30
4	4	8	12	16	20	24	28	32	36	40
5	5	10	15	20	25	30	35	40	45	50
6	6	12	18	24	30	36	42	48	54	60
7	7	14	21	28	35	42	49	56	63	70
8	8	16	24	32	40	48	56	64	72	80
9	9	18	27	36	45	54	63	72	81	90
10	10	20	30	40	50	60	70	80	90	100

Pg 27

1.

X	4	5	6
6	24	30	36
5	20	25	30
4	16	20	24
3	12	15	18
2	8	10	12

2.

X	0	6	8	4	9
5	0	30	40	20	45
4	0	24	32	16	36
3	0	18	24	12	27

3.

X	2	3	4	5	6
10	20	30	40	50	60
11	22	33	44	55	66
12	24	36	48	60	72

X	5	4	3
6	30	24	18
5	25	20	15
4	20	16	12
3	15	12	9
2	10	8	6

4.

Pg 28		Pg 29		Pg 30	
No.	Answer	No.	Answer	No.	Answer
1	260	1	1,968	1	735
2	147	2	3,168	2	1,536
3	108	3	432	3	1,944
4	552	4	1,944	4	3,216
5	456	5	2,088	5	5,525
6	392	6	1,036	6	3,404
7	116	7	935	7	3,354
8	160	8	2,046	8	1,015
9	476	9	1,656	9	3,196
10	747	10	288	10	1,800
				11	2,916
				12	5,568
				13	2,666
				14	8,740
				15	1,638
				16	7,200
				17	1,260
				18	6,566
				19	2,128
				20	3,705

Pg 31		Pg 32		Pg 33	
No.	Answer	No.	Answer	No.	Answer
1	42	1	7,383	1	25,532
2	640	2	4,921	2	28,896
3	57	3	22,016	3	36,096
4	72	4	16,524	4	11,713
		5	15,200	5	41,724
		6	24,999	6	40,807
		7	33,418	7	8,668
		8	5,640	8	15,876
		9	21,204	9	9,164
		10	53,952	10	31,178
		11	74,036	11	9,924
		12	37,905	12	18,278
		13	23,970	13	63,264
		14	50,007	14	45,689
		15	47,288	15	37,944
		16	45,045	16	22,743
		17	60,800	17	67,425
		18	57,072	18	14,314
		19	26,826	19	52,500
		20	83,040	20	63,624

Pg 34		Pg 35		Pg 36	
No.	Answer	No.	Answer	No.	Answer
1	3,381	1	77,532	1	31,572
2	956	2	102,915	2	68,740
3	1,536	3	167,684	3	152,875
4	608	4	253,425	4	32,147
		5	90,364	5	134,096
		6	376,467	6	174,801
		7	296,472	7	59,496
		8	230,278	8	226,023
		9	156,581	9	51,940
		10	254,910	10	128,808
		11	238,908	11	465,519
		12	404,247	12	382,932
		13	174,135	13	207,900
		14	606,268	14	641,056
		15	291,712	15	579,198
		16	260,559	16	269,244
		17	718,650	17	196,174
		18	524,688	18	793,945
		19	116,795	19	561,000
		20	488,166	20	885,024

Pg 37		Pg 38		Pg 39	
No.	Answer	No.	Answer	No.	Answer
1	157,680	1	66,794	1	418,284
2	222,221	2	69,689	2	250,355
3	79,530	3	258,937	3	584,168
4	269,346	4	128,853	4	826,428
5	63,784	5	230,955	5	1,660,480
6	120,825	6	130,104	6	1,604,106
7	568,874	7	180,048	7	785,436
8	182,400	8	103,170	8	588,707
9	145,148	9	350,966	9	1,668,172
10	616,710	10	247,648	10	1,940,352
11	110,670	11	140,140	11	3,672,774
12	106,524	12	101,106	12	1,145,224
13	308,355	13	203,109	13	555,182
14	445,060	14	285,950	14	3,315,922
15	473,324	15	104,328	15	3,198,804
		16	273,456	16	2,714,376
		17	180,560	17	4,070,924
		18	193,400	18	5,319,210
		19	87,269	19	5,624,400
		20	582,556	20	6,151,680

Pg 40		Pg 41	
No.	Answer	No.	Answer
1	2,133,216	1	6^4
2	345,555	2	3^3
3	1,143,539	3	5^3
4	1,110,444	4	7^4
5	2,901,440	5	9^5
6	2,880,279	6	8^6
7	1,093,680	7	2^6
8	855,218	8	4^4
9	1,770,131	9	5^3
10	1,327,798	10	6^5
11	4,844,560	11	7^7
12	1,395,384	12	2^3
13	3,455,694	13	3^4
14	630,343	14	9^6
15	1,953,252		
16	1,192,296		
17	5,038,836		
18	782,760		
19	8,052,375		
20	3,588,480		

Pg 42	
No.	Answer
1	9 x 9 x 9 = 729
2	5 x 5 x 5 x 5 x 5 = 3,125
3	8 x 8 x 8 x 8 = 4,096
4	2 x 2 x 2 x 2 x 2 x 2 x 2 x 2 x 2 = 512
5	6 x 6 x 6 x 6 = 1,296
6	4 x 4 x 4 x 4 x 4 = 1,024

Pg 43	
No.	Answer
1	8 x 8 = 64
2	6 x 6 x 6 x 6 x 6 = 7,776
3	7 x 7 x 7 x 7 = 2,401
4	3 x 3 x 3 x 3 x 3 x 3 x 3 x 3 = 6,561
5	4 x 4 x 4 = 64
6	5 x 5 x 5 x 5 x 5 = 3,125

Pg 44	
No.	Answer
1	9 < 16
2	64 > 9
3	16 < 25
4	7,776 > 64
5	27 > 25
6	125 > 49
7	4,096 > 125
8	216 < 729
9	256 < 4,096
10	25 < 81
11	343 > 4
12	256 > 9
13	512 > 16
14	81 < 729
15	36 < 49

Chapter 3 – Division

Pg 47 No.	Answer	Pg 48 No.	Answer	Pg 49 No.	Answer	Pg 50 No.	Answer
1	16 r 1	1	13 r 2	1	8 trips	1	367 r 1
2	7 r 3	2	12 r 3	2	5 days	2	297 r 1
3	12 r 5	3	17 r 2	3	7 apples	3	134
4	45 r 1	4	10 r 2	4	9 cookies		
5	24 r 3	5	39				
6	14 r 2	6	11 r 3				
7	11 r 3	7	14 r 3				
8	33 r 1	8	21 r 1				
		9	15 r 1				
		10	41 r 1				
		11	10 r 7				
		12	12 r 5				

Pg 51 No.	Answer	Pg 52 No.	Answer	Pg 53 No.	Answer
1	153 r 2	1	65 r 7	1	1,241 r 2
2	32	2	68 r 4	2	569 r 5
3	196	3	129 r 4	3	1,522 r 1
4	139 r 2	4	338 r 1	4	630 r 1
5	90 r 5	5	21 r 2	5	1,325 r 3
6	148 r 4	6	250	6	2,178 r 3
7	188	7	104 r 1	7	632
8	148 r 1	8	122 r 6	8	968 r 1
9	207 r 1	9	37 r 4	9	450 r 4
10	232 r 2	10	275 r 2	10	1,867 r 1
11	111 r 1	11	113 r 1	11	1,142 r 2
12	140 r 6	12	368	12	999 r 3
13	423	13	84 r 12		
14	44 r 2	14	25		
15	204	15	87 r 1		
16	138	16	95 r 3		
17	192 r 2	17	453 r 1		
18	69 r 4	18	83 r 3		
19	75 r 6	19	97 r 2		
20	149 r 3	20	157		

Pg 54		Pg 55		Pg 56	
No.	Answer	No.	Answer	No.	Answer
1	8,447 r 3	1	4540 r 3	1	52 Hours
2	21,624	2	15,337 r 3	2	13 Days
3	7,325 r 1	3	2,160 r 3	3	51 Hours
4	44,652 r 1	4	8,502 r 4	4	119 Sections
5	7,338 r 6	5	32,380 r 1		
6	18,027 r 4	6	10,381 r 4		
7	9,025	7	24,623 r 2		
8	18,327	8	10,136 r 7		
9	19,560 r 1	9	13,302		
10	4,050 r 6	10	8,324 r 3		
11	16,634 r 3	11	3,439 r 5		
12	7,800 r 7	12	14,152 r 4		

Pg 57		Pg 58		Pg 59	
No.	Answer	No.	Answer	No.	Answer
1	21 r 8	1	22 r 5	1	207
2	19 r 10	2	24 r 18	2	148 r 6
3	20 r 9	3	20 r 9	3	137 r 40
4	37 r 5	4	5 r 4	4	111 r 27
5	15 r 24	5	43 r 1	5	226 r 12
6	13 r 24	6	22 r 7	6	259 r 11
7	16 r 16	7	22 r 4	7	213 r 14
8	12 r 9	8	22 r 9	8	291 r 3
9	10 r 53	9	21 r 20	9	203 r 30
10	19 r 19	10	17 r 8	10	118 r 3
		11	10 r 22	11	161 r 17
		12	10 r 26	12	205 r 10
		13	28 r 9		
		14	38 r 5		
		15	23 r 8		
		16	15 r 15		
		17	3		
		18	18 r 3		
		19	7 r 5		
		20	2 r 63		

Pg 60		Pg 61	
No.	Answer	No.	Answer
1	3,229 r 8	1	2,280 r 6
2	2,502 r 29	2	2,268 r 10
3	1,686 r 32	3	1,278 r 3
4	2,237 r 20	4	1,055 r 13
5	2,122 r 17	5	1,357 r 21
6	585 r 7	6	1,189 r 81
7	3,018 r 23	7	459 r 12
8	1,791 r 26	8	1,029 r 5
9	543 r 35	9	1,345 r 15
10	1,057 r 63	10	942 r 87
11	1,128 r 11	11	1,050 r 35
12	1,629 r 9	12	1,113 r 9

Pg 63		Pg 64	
No.	Answer	No.	Answer
1	$\dfrac{13}{15}$	1	$\dfrac{21}{73}$
2	$\dfrac{23}{37}$	2	$\dfrac{7}{28}$
3	$\dfrac{49}{80}$	3	$\dfrac{22}{89}$
4	$\dfrac{100}{109}$	4	$\dfrac{20}{146}$
5	$\dfrac{30}{64}$	5	$\dfrac{114}{634}$
6	$\dfrac{14}{21}$	6	$\dfrac{4}{12}$
7	$\dfrac{383}{865}$	7	$\dfrac{283}{759}$
8	$\dfrac{33}{55}$	8	$\dfrac{26}{56}$
9	$\dfrac{10}{13}$	9	$\dfrac{79}{207}$
10	$\dfrac{45}{74}$	10	$\dfrac{13}{49}$
11	$\dfrac{238}{250}$	11	$\dfrac{167}{277}$
12	$\dfrac{7}{94}$	12	$\dfrac{238}{534}$
		13	$\dfrac{66}{88}$
		14	$\dfrac{39}{129}$
		15	$\dfrac{189}{952}$

Pg 65	
No.	**Answer**
1	Tomatoes: $\frac{13}{28}$ Eggplants: $\frac{6}{28}$ Potatoes: $\frac{9}{28}$
2	Blue Jays: $\frac{3}{15}$ Sparrows: $\frac{9}{15}$ Ducks: $\frac{6}{15}$ Eagles: $\frac{1}{15}$
3	Bass: $\frac{2}{17}$ Trout: $\frac{6}{17}$ Guppies: $\frac{5}{17}$ Goldfish: $\frac{4}{17}$
4	Hamburgers: $\frac{15}{76}$ Chicken Wings: $\frac{22}{76}$ Sausages: $\frac{39}{76}$

Pg 66

$$\frac{1}{4}$$ $$=$$ $$\frac{2}{8}$$

$$\frac{2}{4}$$ $$=$$ $$\frac{4}{8}$$

$$\frac{3}{8}$$ $$=$$ $$\frac{6}{16}$$

$$\frac{5}{8}$$ $$=$$ $$\frac{10}{16}$$

Pg 67		Pg 68		Pg 69	
No.	Answer	No.	Answer	No.	Answer
1	$\frac{9}{9}, \frac{2}{3}$	1	$\frac{3}{5}, \frac{4}{5}$	1	$\frac{5}{7} + \frac{2}{7} = \frac{7}{7}$
2	$\frac{4}{4}, \frac{1}{3}$	2	$\frac{4}{6}, \frac{5}{6}$	2	$\frac{1}{5} + \frac{2}{5} = \frac{3}{5}$
3	$\frac{5}{5}, \frac{4}{7}$	3	$\frac{3}{7}, \frac{5}{7}$	3	$\frac{7}{10} + \frac{2}{10} = \frac{9}{10}$
4	$\frac{3}{3}, \frac{3}{8}$	4	$\frac{3}{8}, \frac{6}{8}$	4	$\frac{10}{12} + \frac{2}{12} = \frac{12}{12}$
5	$\frac{3}{3}, \frac{5}{7}$	5	$\frac{3}{5}, \frac{2}{5}$	5	$\frac{2}{9} + \frac{3}{9} = \frac{5}{9}$
6	$\frac{8}{8}, \frac{2}{5}$	6	$\frac{3}{4}, \frac{2}{4}$	6	$\frac{5}{7} + \frac{2}{7} = \frac{7}{7}$
7	$\frac{5}{5}, \frac{2}{5}$	7	$\frac{5}{7}, \frac{2}{7}$	7	$\frac{6}{9} + \frac{1}{9} = \frac{7}{9}$
8	$\frac{4}{4}, \frac{4}{9}$	8	$\frac{8}{9}, \frac{4}{9}$	8	$\frac{9}{12} + \frac{2}{12} = \frac{11}{12}$
9	$\frac{6}{6}, \frac{2}{5}$			9	$\frac{6}{7} + \frac{4}{7} = \frac{10}{7}$
10	$\frac{9}{9}, \frac{1}{3}$			10	$\frac{7}{8} + \frac{1}{8} = \frac{8}{8}$
11	$\frac{2}{2}, \frac{4}{7}$			11	$\frac{3}{9} + \frac{5}{9} = \frac{8}{9}$
12	$\frac{16}{16}, \frac{1}{2}$			12	$\frac{9}{10} + \frac{7}{10} = \frac{16}{10}$

Pg 70		Pg 71		Pg 72	
No.	Answer	No.	Answer	No.	Answer
1	$\frac{12}{18} - \frac{4}{18} = \frac{8}{18}$	1	$\frac{2}{2}$	1	12
2	$\frac{4}{7} - \frac{1}{7} = \frac{3}{7}$	2	$\frac{3}{3}$	2	12
3	$\frac{7}{9} - \frac{4}{9} = \frac{3}{9}$	3	$\frac{4}{4}$	3	10
4	$\frac{4}{5} - \frac{3}{5} = \frac{1}{5}$	4	$\frac{3}{3}$	4	40
5	$\frac{3}{7} - \frac{2}{7} = \frac{1}{7}$	5	$\frac{8}{8}$	5	5
6	$\frac{6}{7} - \frac{5}{7} = \frac{1}{7}$	6	$\frac{5}{5}$	6	90
7	$\frac{9}{9} - \frac{6}{9} = \frac{3}{9}$	7	$\frac{3}{3}$	7	80
8	$\frac{8}{9} - \frac{3}{9} = \frac{5}{9}$	8	$\frac{11}{11}$	8	16
9	$\frac{6}{7} - \frac{3}{7} = \frac{3}{7}$	9	$\frac{9}{9}$	9	28
10	$\frac{8}{9} - \frac{2}{9} = \frac{6}{9}$			10	90
11	$\frac{5}{6} - \frac{2}{6} = \frac{3}{6}$			11	14
12	$\frac{8}{9} - \frac{5}{9} = \frac{3}{9}$			12	55
				13	128
				14	15
				15	50
				16	80
				17	12
				18	15
				19	6
				20	16

Pg 73		Pg 74	
No.	Answer	No.	Answer
1	$\frac{4}{8}+\frac{1}{8}=\frac{5}{8}$	1	$\frac{10}{20}-\frac{6}{20}=\frac{4}{20}$
2	$\frac{4}{12}+\frac{6}{12}=\frac{10}{12}$	2	$\frac{14}{15}-\frac{12}{15}=\frac{2}{15}$
3	$\frac{6}{21}+\frac{5}{21}=\frac{11}{21}$	3	$\frac{13}{18}-\frac{6}{18}=\frac{7}{18}$
4	$\frac{4}{28}+\frac{21}{28}=\frac{25}{28}$	4	$\frac{35}{40}-\frac{20}{40}=\frac{15}{40}$
5	$\frac{30}{50}+\frac{12}{50}=\frac{42}{50}$	5	$\frac{40}{48}-\frac{29}{48}=\frac{11}{48}$
6	$\frac{6}{24}+\frac{15}{24}=\frac{21}{24}$	6	$\frac{16}{24}-\frac{15}{24}=\frac{1}{24}$
7	$\frac{21}{48}+\frac{16}{48}=\frac{37}{48}$	7	$\frac{36}{49}-\frac{21}{49}=\frac{15}{49}$
8	$\frac{45}{81}+\frac{12}{81}=\frac{57}{81}$	8	$\frac{45}{54}-\frac{29}{54}=\frac{16}{54}$
9	$\frac{9}{36}+\frac{18}{36}=\frac{27}{36}$	9	$\frac{63}{81}-\frac{54}{81}=\frac{9}{81}$
10	$\frac{28}{63}+\frac{5}{63}=\frac{33}{63}$	10	$\frac{54}{63}-\frac{35}{63}=\frac{19}{63}$
11	$\frac{39}{72}+\frac{24}{72}=\frac{63}{72}$	11	$\frac{27}{48}-\frac{24}{48}=\frac{3}{48}$
12	$\frac{17}{56}+\frac{35}{56}=\frac{52}{56}$	12	$\frac{70}{100}-\frac{50}{100}=\frac{20}{100}$

	Pg 75
No.	**Answer**
1	$5\dfrac{10}{12}$
2	$6\dfrac{4}{9}$
3	$7\dfrac{4}{5}$
4	$2\dfrac{20}{23}$
5	$13\dfrac{6}{8}$
6	$13\dfrac{10}{15}$
7	$13\dfrac{30}{39}$
8	$12\dfrac{9}{10}$
9	$4\dfrac{5}{19}$
10	$3\dfrac{5}{8}$
11	$3\dfrac{6}{16}$
12	$5\dfrac{4}{6}$
13	$5\dfrac{4}{25}$
14	$11\dfrac{1}{10}$
15	$8\dfrac{27}{44}$

Pg 76		Pg 77	
No.	Answer	No.	Answer
1	$5\frac{5}{10} = 5\frac{1}{2}$	1	$\frac{13}{3}$
2	$9\frac{9}{12} = 9\frac{3}{4}$	2	$\frac{38}{4}$
3	$9\frac{6}{18} = 9\frac{1}{3}$	3	$\frac{13}{2}$
4	$8\frac{4}{8} = 8\frac{1}{2}$	4	$\frac{32}{5}$
5	$12\frac{12}{24} = 12\frac{1}{2}$	5	$\frac{95}{10}$
6	$15\frac{18}{36} = 15\frac{1}{2}$	6	$\frac{21}{5}$
7	$11\frac{21}{56} = 11\frac{3}{8}$	7	$\frac{25}{7}$
8	$14\frac{45}{81} = 14\frac{5}{9}$	8	$\frac{14}{3}$
9	$3\frac{8}{16} = 3\frac{1}{2}$	9	$\frac{26}{5}$
10	$12\frac{4}{12} = 12\frac{1}{3}$	10	$\frac{30}{3}$
11	$8\frac{14}{28} = 8\frac{1}{2}$	11	$\frac{27}{5}$
12	$12\frac{6}{9} = 12\frac{2}{3}$	12	$\frac{18}{8}$
13	$39\frac{28}{42} = 39\frac{2}{3}$	13	$\frac{52}{5}$
14	$18\frac{18}{63} = 18\frac{2}{7}$	14	$\frac{27}{3}$
15	$25\frac{12}{21} = 25\frac{4}{7}$	15	$\frac{69}{11}$
16	$11\frac{20}{50} = 11\frac{2}{5}$	16	$\frac{16}{3}$
		17	$\frac{37}{22}$
		18	$\frac{24}{9}$
		19	$\frac{34}{4}$
		20	$\frac{32}{3}$

Pg 78	
No.	Answer
1	7
2	4
3	3
4	9
5	8
6	31
7	5
8	42
9	$2\frac{3}{6}$
10	$2\frac{2}{4}$
11	$3\frac{1}{2}$
12	$2\frac{3}{8}$
13	$5\frac{3}{4}$
14	$8\frac{2}{3}$
15	$5\frac{5}{9}$
16	$5\frac{6}{8}$

Chapter 5 – Decimals

Pg 80		Pg 81		Pg 82		Pg 83	
No.	Answer	No.	Answer	No.	Answer	No.	Answer
1	10.83	1	19.44	1	40.365	1	971.2
2	11.55	2	17.82	2	16.728	2	522.16
3	17.01	3	18.61	3	108.352	3	233.49
4	74.83	4	22.83	4	13.774	4	480.18
5	71.38	5	264.57	5	68.174	5	1,535.15
6	71.22	6	85.62	6	131.437	6	856.17
		7	93.31	7	109.184	7	839.27
		8	115.88	8	116.236	8	829.72
		9	1,000.77	9	77.166	9	1,019.78

Pg 84		Pg 85	
No.	Answer	No.	Answer
1	points: 75.4 rebounds: 16.2	1	165.93
2	18.5	2	130.62
3	19.55	3	337.26
4	40.34	4	443.47
		5	898.79
		6	1,328.24
		7	913.05
		8	1,676.61
		9	98.011
		10	47.257
		11	134.537
		12	110.116
		13	752.03
		14	1,591.924
		15	1,292.80
		16	675.154
		17	1,161.326
		18	1,130.321
		19	1,107.368
		20	1,526.574

Pg 86		Pg 87		Pg 88		Pg 89	
No.	Answer	No.	Answer	No.	Answer	No.	Answer
1	2,292.203	1	8,947.33	1	4.55	1	49.97
2	1,024.508	2	14,437.96	2	13.45	2	27.68
3	2,369.367	3	10,098.36	3	27.4	3	13.89
4	1,589.946	4	9,065.53	4	559.93	4	15.96
5	1,602.404	5	20,055.64	5	88.65	5	1.17
6	2,443.596	6	14,216.45	6	298.91	6	30.6
7	2,241.336	7	12,316.47			7	18.17
8	1,953.052	8	8,814.81			8	46.75
9	1,862.583	9	10,754.98			9	17.56
10	2,328.303	10	13,061.62				
11	1,192.89	11	10,903.89				
12	2,315.809	12	11,889.87				
13	3,293.375	13	23,148.84				
14	2,686.997	14	12,299.29				
15	2,241.406	15	10,762.47				
16	2,921.589	16	23,018.72				

Pg 90		Pg 91		Pg 92		Pg 93	
No.	Answer	No.	Answer	No.	Answer	No.	Answer
1	592.45	1	79.312	1	49.33	1	883.23
2	802.22	2	36.252	2	326.39	2	2,100.45
3	293.5	3	55.411	3	105.26	3	4,459.81
4	37.64	4	60.407	4	123.73	4	2,713.83
5	112.21	5	11.221	5	241.84	5	5,062.25
6	466.93	6	338.301	6	341.48	6	7,294.40
7	499.62	7	16.151	7	347.08	7	5,944.50
8	103.94	8	6.905	8	169.62	8	1,416.89
9	279.49	9	579.732	9	534.35	9	2,339.55
				10	465.36	10	4,778.22
				11	87.14	11	2,424.61
				12	33.44	12	1,172.31
				13	44.791	13	452.891
				14	20.014	14	632.574
				15	13.269	15	626.454
				16	5.9	16	316.231
				17	21.28	17	94.845
				18	36.574	18	202.634
				19	42.545	19	153.408
				20	25.487	20	561.034

Pg 94		Pg 95		Pg 96		Pg 97	
No.	Answer	No.	Answer	No.	Answer	No.	Answer
1	17.3123	1	1.35	1	$152.40	1	$519.58
2	39.8811	2	26.82	2	$328.14	2	$333.97
3	21.4554	3	53.96	3	$387.76	3	$777.29
4	45.6271	4	2.41	4	$227.07	4	$642.55
5	164.069			5	$447.00	5	$928.53
6	168.894			6	$1,433.61	6	$1,528.24
7	20.514			7	$585.61	7	$1,213.41
8	109.208			8	$1,281.75	8	$1,605.84
9	10,213.10			9	$889.47	9	$702.13
10	1,588.44			10	$1,343.92	10	$1,236.92
11	6,203.53			11	$771.90	11	$1,142.83
12	5.35945			12	$1,076.38	12	$978.09
13	2,176.26			13	$1,452.60	13	$2,496.52
14	202.851			14	$1,132.89	14	$2,007.13
15	2.03419			15	$1,109.55	15	$2,701.26
16	12.2159			16	$882.25	16	$2,751.54
17	74,083.40					17	1,364.77
18	20,618.30					18	$1,139.83
19	13,601.50					19	$1,405.49
20	1,078.77					20	$1,875.55

Pg 98		Pg 99		Pg 100		Pg 101	
No.	Answer	No.	Answer	No.	Answer	No.	Answer
1	$2.38	1	$167.57	1	53.12	1	22.737
2	$3.35	2	$235.72	2	9.57	2	5.891
3	$1.85	3	$221.39	3	29.48	3	4.446
4	$2.47	4	$205.16	4	21.24	4	34.368
5	$5.31	5	$335.66	5	13.05	5	19.032
6	$1.79	6	$685.64	6	56.95	6	27.36
7	$3.82	7	$141.12	7	13.23	7	35.336
8	$4.63	8	$65.73	8	60.76	8	1,440.60
9	$2.86	9	$213.18	9	44.66	9	8.2917
10	$2.14	10	$508.08	10	77.9	10	194.88
11	$1.75	11	$62.57	11	65.12	11	.24153
12	$4.22	12	$671.71	12	33.63	12	995.9
13	$59.09	13	$275.12	13	30.38	13	32.074
14	$104.35	14	$488.63	14	10.75	14	293.26
15	$76.62	15	$34.40	15	33.93	15	6.6744
16	$222.33	16	$524.21			16	185.52
17	$451.09	17	$212.65			17	2.058
18	$321.63	18	$175.49			18	223.29
19	$441.51	19	$248.53			19	5,603.40
20	$82.86	20	$216.79			20	4.0736
						21	31.524
						22	395.34
						23	26.978
						24	19.91
						25	442.96

Pg 102		Pg 103	
No.	Answer	No.	Answer
1	124.576	1	938.448
2	14.5497	2	357.7665
3	1,656.86	3	449.709
4	167.678	4	1.831536
5	42.526	5	5696.46
6	14.1327	6	1,242.448
7	340.548	7	318.8694
8	110.451	8	304.3408
9	927.5	9	1,371.806
10	24.2934	10	404.9125
11	7303.12	11	248.5998
12	1,762.18	12	27,895.43
13	360.549	13	86.8795
14	509.819	14	185.8618
15	270.338	15	257.2271
16	262.145	16	54,917.25
17	1,653.75	17	624.9639
18	78.4101	18	6,041.386
19	55.062	19	107.1348
20	192.576	20	41,661.18
21	8,360.52		
22	8,045.73		
23	35.1978		
24	27.6216		
25	745.129		

Chapter 6 – Geometry

No.	Pg 108 Answer	No.	Pg 109 Answer
1	74 x 74 = 5,476 in.^{2}	1	11in. x 6in. ÷ 2 = 33 in.^{2}
2	134ft. x 749ft. = 100,366 ft.^{2}	2	12ft. x 17ft. ÷ 2 = 102 ft.^{2}
3	205in. x 205in. = 42,025 in.^{2}	3	5in. x 14in. ÷ 2 = 35 in.^{2}
4	299ft. x 436ft. = 130,364 ft.^{2}	4	75in. x 46in. ÷ 2 =1,72 5in.^{2}
5	637in. x 637in. = 405,769 in.^{2}	5	94in. x 89in. ÷ 2 = 4,183 in.^{2}
6	507yd. x 1,262yd. = 639,834 yd.^{2}	6	112ft. x 156ft. ÷ 2 = 8,736 ft.^{2}

No.	Pg 110 Answer	No.	Pg 111 Answer
1	6 x 6 = 36 ft.^{2}	1	6 + 9 x 6 ÷ 2 = 45 yds.^{2}
2	13 x 5 = 65 in.^{2}	2	24 + 16 x 8 ÷ 2 = 160 ft.^{2}
3	15 x 17 = 255 ft.^{2}	3	20 + 32 x 12 ÷ 2 = 312 in.^{2}
4	75 x 45 = 3,375 ft.^{2}	4	55 + 110 x 40 ÷ 2 = 3,300 ft.^{2}
5	136 x 115 = 15,640 in.^{2}	5	136 + 175 x 212 ÷ 2 = 32,966 in.^{2}
6	563 x 599 = 337,237 ft.^{2}	6	250 + 210 x 88 ÷ 2 = 20,240 in.^{2}

No.	Pg 112 Answer	No.	Pg 113 Answer
1	55 + 36 + 42 + 67 = 197 yd.	1	12 + 4 + 4 + 6 + 8 + 10 = 44 yd.
2	125 + 89 + 89 + 125 = 428 ft.	2	4 + 13 + 1 + 12 + 15 = 45 ft.
3	123 + 215 + 107 + 324 = 769 in.	3	88 + 200 + 96 + 88 + 105 + 88 + 411 = 1,076 in.
4	75 + 347 + 62 + 289 +101 = 874 ft.	4	8 + 8 + 8 + 8 + 8 + 8 + 8 + 8 = 64 ft.
5	572 + 635 + 468 = 1,675 in.	5	20 + 20 + 5 + 15 + 15 + 5 = 80 in.
6	917 + 234 + 705 + 917 = 2,773 yd.	6	35 + 4 + 17 + 20 + 19 + 15 + 4 = 114 in.
		7	60 + 55 + 34 + 27 + 10 = 186 ft.
		8	7 + 18 + 19 + 7 + 22 + 8 + 23 = 104 in.
		9	100 + 100 + 25 + 25 + 27 + 50 + 25 = 352 yd.

Pg 114

No.	Answer
1	vertex- 1, ray- 2, point- 3
2	vertex-1, line segment-2, point -5
3	line-1, ray-2, point-2
4	line-1, ray-2, vertex-1, point-2
5	ray-3, vertex-2, point-4
6	ray-1, line segment-1, vertex-1, point-4
7	ray- 3, vertex-2, point-4
8	ray-2, line-2, point-2

Pg 115

No.	Answer		
1	Angle: ABC	Vertex: B	Rays: AB, CB
2	Angle: 123	Vertex: 2	Rays: 12, 23
3	Angle: QRS	Vertex: R	Rays: SR, QR
4	Angle: XYZ	Vertex: Y	Rays: XY, YZ
5	Angle: 456	Vertex: 5	Rays: 45, 56
6	Angle: EFG	Vertex: F	Rays: EF, EG
7	Angle: MNO	Vertex: N	Rays: MN, NO
8	Angle: 678	Vertex: 7	Rays: 67, 78
9	Angle: DEF	Vertex: E	Rays: FE, DE
10	Angle: 789	Vertex: 8	Rays: 78, 89
11	Angle: 012	Vertex: 1	Rays: 01, 12
12	Angle: UVW	Vertex: V	Rays: UV, VW

Pg 117

1. Pyramid
    a. 4
    b. 6
    c. 4

2. Cylinder
    a. 0
    b. 2
    c. 3

3. Cube
    a. 8
    b. 12
    c. 6

Pg 118

1. Cone
    a. 1
    b. 1
    c. 2

2. Cuboid
    a. 8
    b. 12
    c. 6

3. Pyramid
    a. 5
    b. 8
    c. 5

Pg 120

No.	Answer		
1	Circle: A	Radius: AB, AC, AD	Diameter: BC
2	Circle: E	Radius: EF, EH, EG	Diameter: FG
3	Circle: X	Radius: XW, XZ, XY	Diameter: WY
4	Circle: R	Radius: RQ, RS,RT	Diameter: QT
5	Circle: M	Radius: ML, MN, MO	Diameter: LO
6	Circle: X	Radius: XR, XA, XP	Diameter: AR

Pg 121

No.	Answer
1	18 ÷ 2 = 9 cm.
2	36 ÷ 2 = 18 in.
3	112 ÷ 2 = 56 ft.
4	388 ÷ 2 = 194 in.
5	956 ÷ 2 = 478 ft.
6	3,624 ÷ 2 = 1,812 cm.

Pg 122

No.	Answer
1	12 x 2 = 24 in.
2	29 x 2 = 58 cm.
3	89 x 2 = 178 ft.
4	113 x 2 = 226 cm.
5	624 x 2 = 1,24 in.
6	2,935x 2 = 5,870 ft.

Pg 123

No.	Answer
1	345.4 in.
2	226.08 cm.
3	942 ft.
4	120.89 ft.
5	3,337.192 in.
6	21.64716 cm.

Chapter 7 - Graphs

Pg 126		Pg 127	
No.	Answer	No.	Answer
1	Game 5	1	60
2	Game 1	2	35
3	52 Goals	3	45
4	4 Goals	4	30
5	7 Goals	5	45
6	16 Goals	6	50
7	25 Goals	7	65
8	Games 2 and 8	8	25
		9	40
		10	20
		11	25
		12	5
		13	25
		14	5
		15	20
		16	30
		17	45
		18	10

Pg 128

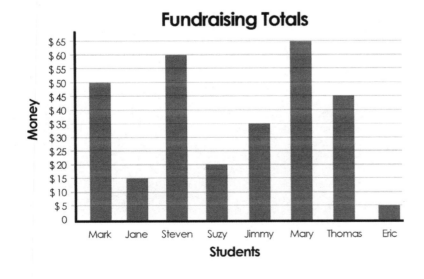

- 43 -

Pg 128	
No.	**Answer**
1	$45
2	$20
3	$15
4	$35
5	$50
6	$60
7	$65
8	$5
9	$55
10	$15
11	$15
12	$45
13	$45
14	$30

Pg 129	
No.	**Answer**
1	2012
2	2011
3	85 degrees
4	50 degrees
5	55 degrees
6	Feb
7	July
8	5 degrees
9	90 degrees
10	60 degrees
11	55 degrees
12	10 degrees
13	Stayed the same
14	2011

Pg 130

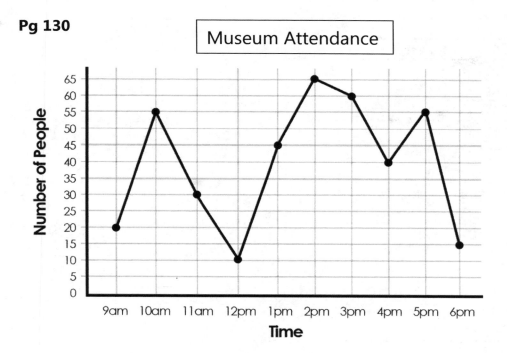

Pg 130	
No.	**Answer**
1	2pm
2	12pm
3	10
4	20
5	40
6	25
7	20
8	40
9	12pm - 1pm
10	5pm - 6pm

Pg 131

No.	Answer
1	A10, C10, C7, E7
2	E10, I10, F7, H7
3	J10, J8, O10, O8
4	Q7, S10, T7
5	A6, A4, B4, B3, D3, D6
6	B2, B1, E5, E2, G5, G1
7	H6, H5, I7, I4, J7, J4, K6, K5
8	I3, I1, L3, O1
9	L7, L4, O5, O4, P7, P6, S6, S5
10	P2, Q4, Q1, S4, S1, T2

Pg 132

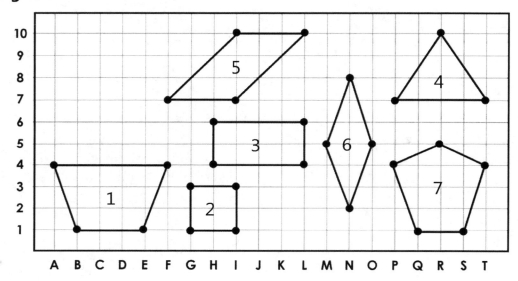

Pg 132

No.	Answer
1	trapezoid
2	square
3	rectangle
4	triangle
5	parallelogram
6	rhombus
7	pentagon

Pg 133		Pg 135	
No.	Answer	No.	Answer
1	Art	1	Tennis shoes
2	Math	2	Tennis shoes
3	Science	3	Tennis shoes
4	Reading	4	Boots
5	Puppies	5	Sandals
6	Fish	6	Tennis shoes
7	Kittens	7	Boots
8	Gerbil	8	Boots
		9	Boots
		10	Sandals

Pg 136

A **pie graph** shows how the parts of something relate to the whole. It is divided into sectors. Each sector represents a particular category. The sum of all the parts will always equal 100%.

Using the information below, fill in the pie graphs with the correct numbers.

Most Studied Planets

1. Mars - 50%

2. Mercury - 6%

3. Venus - 10%

4. Neptune - 34%

How Students Get to School

1. Shool Bus - 42%

2. Car - 35%

3. Bike - 15%

4. Walk - 8%

Favorite Movie Types in Schools

1. Comedy - 35%

2. Action - 18%

3. Drama - 8%

4. Animation - 24%

5. Science Fiction- 15%

Fish Population in the Pond

1. Bass - 20%

2. Catfish - 27%

3. Trout - 14%

4. Guppies - 32%

5. Turtles - 7%

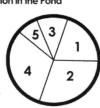

- 47 -

Practice Test Answers

Practice Test #1

Answers and Explanations

1. A: The digit 5 is in the 5th column, which is the ten thousands column. Therefore the digit represents the value 50,000.

2. C: Robinson has the highest number of points. The number of goals and assists need to be added to determine this.

Player	Goals	Assists	Points
Phillips	2	23	25
Jackson	5	17	22
Robinson	13	15	28
Miller	8	19	27

3. B: $\frac{15}{4}$. The value of 3 is equivalent to $\frac{12}{4}$. Therefore, $3\frac{3}{4} = \frac{12}{4} + \frac{3}{4} = \frac{15}{4}$. Another way of

of finding this is sometimes called the "C" method. $3\frac{3}{4}$ equals $\frac{4\times3+3}{4} = \frac{15}{4}$.

4. C: The largest multiple of 12 less than 151 is 144. This means there are $151 - 144 = 7$ eggs left over.

5. C: Count from the 3: tenths, hundredths, thousandths.

6. D: A diagram of the plot would look like this:

W=8m

L=3W=24 m

The perimeter of a rectangle is the formula $P = 2L + 2W$ which produces $2(24) + 2(8) = 48 + 16 = 64\ m$.

7. Part A: B: The pattern in the table is that the number of customers is increasing by 25 each week. This means that there should be $205 + 25 = 230$ customers expected in week 4.

Week	Customers
1	155
2	180
3	205
4	230

+25

+25

+25

Part B: $2760: From Part A you know there will be 230 people in week 4. If each meal is $12 then just multiply to get the answer. $230 \times 12 = 2760$

8. 3: The area of a rectangular prism is $A = L \times W \times H$. The problem gives L, W, and A. To get H just divide A by L and W. $144 \div 8 = 18 \div 6 = 3$. So $H=3$.

9. A: This is a simple subtraction problem with decimals. Line up the decimals and subtract 9 from 8. Since this can't be done, borrow 10 from the 5. Cross out the 5 and make it 4. Now subtract 9 from 18 to get 9. Subtract 3 from 4 and get 1. Place the decimal point before the 1.

10. D: The recipe is being multiplied by 4 in this problem, therefore $\frac{1}{8} = \frac{4}{32}$ so a total of 4 cups of milk are needed. Since this is not one of the choices, a conversion is needed. 1 pint = 2 cups and 1 quart = 2 pints, therefore 1 quart = 4 cups.

11. A: To solve a problem like this first find a least common denominator. For 2, 4, and 5 that would be 20. Then convert each fraction to twentieths. $\frac{2}{5} = \frac{8}{20}, \frac{3}{4} = \frac{15}{20}$, and $\frac{1}{2} = \frac{10}{20}$. Next perform the operations that were given. $\frac{8}{20} + \frac{15}{20} - \frac{10}{20} = \frac{13}{20}$.

12. A: To solve, test each answer. Notice that in (A), the numerator has been multiplied by 3 to get 12. The denominator has been multiplied by 3 to get 21. In (B) the numerator has been multiplied by 4 and the denominator has been multiplied by 5. In (C), the numerator has been multiplied by 3 and the denominator has been multiplied by 4. In (D), the numerator has been multiplied by 4 and the denominator has been multiplied by a number less than 4.

13. 10.92: $A = L \times W$, so multiplying $4.2 \times 2.6 = 10.92$. The area of the card is 10.92 sq inches.

14. B: The total number of Evercell batteries is $(4 \times E)$ and the total number of Durapower batteries is $(6 \times D)$. The sum of the two is the total number of batteries in the store.

15. 3.08: To find the total distance multiply the number of laps times the distance of one lap. $11 \times .28 = 3.08$

16. .375, .71, .85: $.3 \times 1.25 = .375$

$1.22 - .85 + .34 = .37 + .34 = .71$

$(.22 + 1.48) \times .5 = (1.7) \times .5 = .85$

17. B: One property of parallelograms is that the opposite sides are parallel. This means $\overline{QS} \parallel \overline{RT}$.

18. A: The rectangular prism volume formula $V = l \times w \times h$ is used here. $210 = 7 \times 5 \times h$. Dividing both sides by 35 gives the answer $h = 6$ inches.

19. Divide the number of yards by 1760, the number of yards in 1 mile. $\frac{18335}{1760} \approx \mathbf{10.42}$ miles.

20. B: There are 36 out of 100 yellow cars in the sample. Since the parking lot has $\frac{1}{4}$ as many cars as the sample, $\frac{1}{4}$ as many yellow cars should be expected.

21. A: $C = \frac{3}{4}(100) + 20$. Since $\frac{1}{4}$ of the original \$100 was sent to the savings account, $\frac{3}{4}$ of the money was kept in cash. The bonus was then added afterward.

22. C: Use approximation to solve this problem quickly: $25 \times \$3 = \$75$. The actual cost to fill the tank was $25.2 \times \$2.98 = \$75.10$.

23. D: The order of operations is parentheses, exponents, multiply, divide, add, subtract. So for this problem it would be: $8 \times (5 - 2) + (4 + 5) = 8 \times 3 + 9 = 24 + 9 = 33$

24. C: Add the 1 hour and 30 minutes to find that Janice finishes her homework at 4:15 PM. Next, add 1 hour and 45 minutes to find that Janice returns home at 6:00 PM.

25. A: The simplest way to compare the two pieces of pie is to find a common dominator for both fractions. The older daughter was given 2/5 of the pie, while the younger daughter was given 1/3 of the pie. The least common dominator for the two fractions is 15. Therefore, the older daughter received 6/15 of the pie and the younger daughter received 5/15 of the pie. 6/15 is larger than 5/15; therefore, the older daughter received a larger slice of the pie.

26. 4.43: When a problem asks for the difference use subtraction. $14.67 - 10.24 = 4.43$.

27. A: Translate the point 5 units to the right and 4 units down to find the location of the lighthouse.

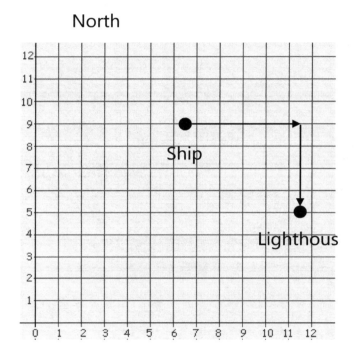

28. D: Plotting the values on a number line demonstrates that this is the only value not in the normal range.

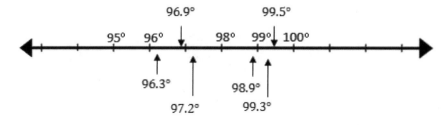

29. B: Use the formula for finding the mean: $\frac{sum\ of\ values}{number\ of\ values}$.
$$\frac{9+16+13+20+22}{5} = \frac{80}{5} = 16.$$

30.

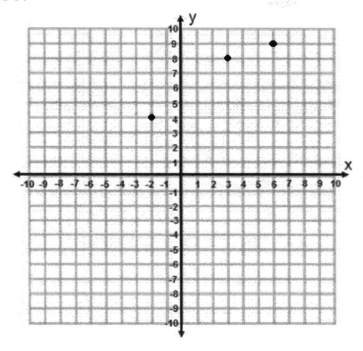

31. B: Divide 92 by 14. $92 \div 14 = 6\,R\,8$. Since 8 is not enough for another team, a total of 6 teams can be formed.

32. Part A: B: By the definition of an isosceles trapezoid, the legs (non-parallel sides) are congruent.

Part B: A: Since the figure is defined as an isosceles, it is known that $\overline{PS}$ and $\overline{QR}$ are parallel and not congruent in length.

33. C:

Expressing $\frac{31}{8} = 3\frac{7}{8}$ makes this easier to see.

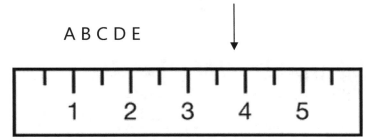

34. C: The points are marked on the figure below.

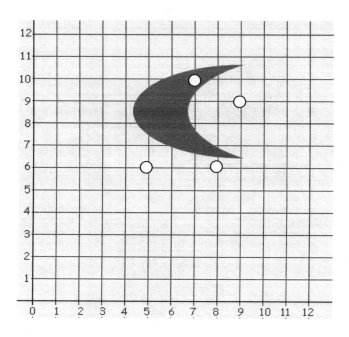

35. C: $1\frac{7}{10}$ is read as one and seven tenths. The 1 can be converted to an equivalent fraction of

$\frac{10}{10}$ and is shown as all ten parts of the first ten section are shaded. $\frac{7}{10}$ indicates that only seven of the ten parts are shaded in the second set of ten. Since the 7 is over the denominator of a ten and read as seven tenths, the seven should be placed in the tenths location when in decimal form. This is the first location to the right of the decimal. The correct decimal form for this is 1.7.

36. $26,150: The total amount they made from T.V.'s is $525 \times 36 = $18,900. The total that they make from game systems is $250 \times 29 = $7,250. $18,900 + $7,250 = $26,150

37. B: Since the probability of being born in the spring or summer is being calculated, the probabilities are added. $\frac{7}{20} + \frac{3}{20} = \frac{10}{20} = \frac{1}{2}$.

38. D: Multiplying the number of weeks by 7 and then adding 5 more days gives the desired result. $7 \times 9 + 5 = 68$.

39. D: To find the difference, subtract. It is important to align decimal places. Note, when subtracting here, the digit in the hundredths place in 0.33 has no digit aligned above it. We must add a zero to 1.5 so that we can align the hundredths places correctly. Now we can subtract 33 hundredths from the 50 hundredths to get 17 hundredths. So, we get 1.17 as our correct answer.

40. B: There are 2 green sections on the spinner and the spinner has 6 sections in all. The probability of spinning green is 2 out of 6, when expressed as a fraction is $\frac{2}{6}$. Written in simplest terms, the fraction is $\frac{1}{3}$.

Practice Test #2

Answers and Explanations

1. D: Fifty-seven thousand is 57,000; adding the three hundred forty to that amount gives the correct answer: 57,340.

2. D: Construct a 3rd column representing improvement. This would be the second score minus the first score for each of the students. David has the greatest improvement of 20 words per minute between the two tests.

Student	First score (words per minute)	Second score (words per minute)	Improvement Second – First scores
Alexander	22	39	17
Betty	39	48	9
Carolyn	27	43	16
David	22	42	20

3. C: The value of 7 is equivalent to $\frac{56}{8}$. Therefore, $7\frac{5}{8} = \frac{56}{8} + \frac{5}{8} = \frac{61}{8}$. Another way of finding this is sometimes called the "C" method: $7\frac{5}{8}$ equals $\frac{8 \times 7 + 5}{8} = \frac{61}{8}$.

4. B: The largest multiple of 12 less than 141 is $12 \times 11 = 132$. This leaves $141 - 132 = 9$ donuts remaining.

5. C: Count from the 5: tenths, hundredths, thousandths.

6. 528: First find Donny's weight in pounds. So, 56-23=33, then it can be converted to ounces by multiplying times 16. $33 \times 16 = 528$.

7. A: Use the area formula for a square: $A = s^2$. Solve the equation: $81 = s^2$, $s = \pm 9$. Since the side of the garden is a length, it must be positive, $s = 9$ feet.

8. B: To solve, test each answer. Notice that in (A), the numerator has been multiplied by 9 to get 18. The denominator has been multiplied by 8. These are not equal fractions. In (C) the numerator has been multiplied by 4 and the denominator has been multiplied by 2. These are not equal fractions. In (D) the numerator has been multiplied by 3 and the denominator has been multiplied by 2. These are not equal fractions. In (B), both numerator and denominator have been multiplied by 4.

9. The hundredths place is the second number after the decimal point. When rounding 1-4 rounds down and 5-9 rounds up.

$3.116 \approx 3.12$

$3.081 \approx 3.08$

$3.006 \approx 3.01$

$3.107 \approx 3.11$

10. D: A trapezoid is a quadrilateral with only one pair of opposite sides parallel.
The other three figures in the problem are a rectangle, a rhombus, and a parallelogram (in that order).

11. B: The proportion given is that 1 gallon of cooking oil will make enough popcorn for 256 people, or 128 ounces serves 256 people. Notice that the amount of oil in ounces needed is exactly one half the number of people being served. This means 48 ounces are needed to serve 96 people. The equivalent amount listed in the choices is 3 pints.

12. B: Working the problem backwards, Jody had $29 before she went to the movies. This was half of the money she made at the bake sale. This means 2 × $29 = $58 was made at the bake sale.

13. A: Since all the answers have a 7 as the whole number, multiply 7 x 14. The answer is 98. The remainder is 1.

14. D: Since the marbles are being equally distributed in 4 equal parts, each friend is simply receiving $\frac{1}{4}$ of the marbles.

15. Part A: 1248: To find the total number of rolls multiply the number of rolls in a package times the number of packages, then times the number of boxes. 8 × 6 × 26 = 1248

Part B: 5: To find out how many shipments they need divide 6100 by 1248. 6100 ÷ 1248 ≈ 4.89. So they would need at least 5 shipments a month.

16. Part A: $\frac{5}{24}$**:** First you need like denominators. For 6 and 8 that would be 24. $\frac{5}{8} = \frac{15}{24}$ and $\frac{5}{6} = \frac{20}{24}$. So, the second one is $\frac{5}{24}$ bigger.

Part B: $2\frac{1}{24}$**:** To find the total you will also need to first find like denominators. In this case 24 will also work. So, $\frac{7}{12} = \frac{14}{24}$, then $\frac{15}{24} + \frac{20}{24} + \frac{14}{24} = \frac{49}{24} = 2\frac{1}{24}$

17. B: By definition, the opposite sides of a parallelogram are equal and congruent.

18. D: Use the volume of a rectangular prism formula $V = L \times W \times H$ to determine the length of the tank.
$$200 = L \times 8 \times 5 \rightarrow 200 = 40L \rightarrow L = 5 \text{ feet.}$$

19. C: Dividing the height of Mt. McKinley by the number of feet in a mile gives the correct result. $\frac{20320}{5280} = 3.85$ miles. This rounds to the approximation of 4 miles high.

20. Using the ratio 8 : 20 and noticing that the school has 12 times more students than the classroom. Multiplying the ratio by 12 gives: **96 : 240**.

21. D: The other choices define A. Raising the wholesale price by $1.75. B. Multiplying the wholesale price by 0.25 and then adding $1.50. C. Multiplying the wholesale price by 1.75.

22. B: Since Laura was leaving the movies at 8:15, go backward 2:45 to get the start time of the movie. 2 hours prior was 6:15, and the additional 45 minutes moves the start time back to 5:30 PM.

23. 48: Order of operations are parentheses, exponents, multiplication, division, addition, and subtraction. The steps to solve this problem are:
$3 + (9 - 4) \times (4 + 5) =?$
$3 + 5 \times 9 =?$
$3 + 45 = 48$

24. B: If you add all of the minutes together you get 202. When converted to hours and minutes that is three hours and 22 minutes.

25. B: Unless the rectangular prism is a cube, some of the sides will have different areas than others. Opposite sides will be equal in area.

26. B: $1\frac{5}{10}$ is read as one and five tenths. The 1 can be converted to an equivalent fraction of

$\frac{10}{10}$ and is shown as all ten parts of the first ten section are shaded. $\frac{5}{10}$ indicates that only
five of the ten parts are shaded in the second set of ten. Since the 5 is over the denominator of a ten and read as five tenths, the five should be placed

in the tenths location when in decimal form. This is the first location to the right of the decimal. The correct decimal form for this is 1.5.

27. B: On the plane provided, north is up and west is to the left. Shift point (8, 5) up 2 and left 4 units to obtain the position of the fire.

North

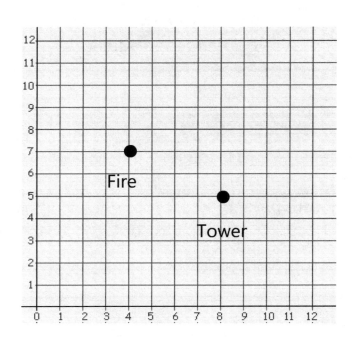

East

28. D: A box that is 13 × 4 × 8 would be 416 cubic inches.

29. C: Use the formula for finding the mean, $mean = \dfrac{sum\ of\ values}{number\ of\ values}$.

$$\frac{22+28+38+48+45}{5} = \frac{180}{5} = 36$$

30. D: If Ice Chest A can hold twice as many drinks as B then that means it can hold 48 drinks. If the larger compartment holds 34 and 48-34=14, then the smaller one holds 14.

31. C: If the average weight of a horse is 1100 lbs, the weight of the horses in the race would be 8 × 1100 = 8800 lbs. Dividing this number by 2000 gives the total weight in tons. $8800\ lbs \times \dfrac{1\ ton}{2000\ lbs} = \dfrac{8800}{2000}\ tons = 4.4\ tons$.

- 60 -

32. The solution is found by finding the whole number part of the quotient when dividing 417 by 18: $417 \div 18 = \textbf{23 R 3}$. Therefore 23 full boxes can be made and 3 pears would be left over.

33. D: A regular pentagon is a 5 sided figure with all sides equal in length. Therefore the perimeter is $5 \times 6.5 = 32.5$ centimeters.

34. C: Convert $\frac{35}{8}$ to a mixed number using division: $\frac{35}{8} = 4\frac{3}{8}$. Point D is located at $4\frac{1}{2}$ inches, so the length is before D. C is 3 inches, so obviously the length is more than C.

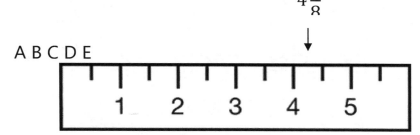

35. B: The four choices are marked on the diagram below.

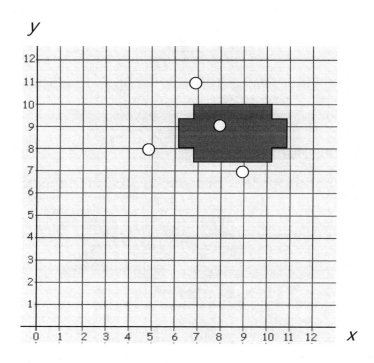

36. C: Since the probability of being either a carpenter or an electrician is being calculated, the probabilities are added. $\frac{13}{50} + \frac{7}{50} = \frac{20}{50} = \frac{2}{5}$.

37. B: This is the only line graph that correctly shows the increase in customers up to 6:00 pm and then the decrease in customers at 8:00 pm.

38. D: To correctly order the numbers in this question, making the decimals all have the same number of digits by adding as many zeros as necessary to the numbers with fewer digits makes them easier to compare. Here, only 17.4 has fewer digits than the others, so add one zero to make it 17.40 (this does not change the value). Now, by comparing place values from left to right of 17.03, 17.4, 17.31, and 17.09, we see that 17.03 is the shortest, 17.09 is the next longest, 17.31 is the third longest, and 17.4 is the longest. Notice the question asked for shortest to longest, not longest to shortest.

39. A: Write 512 then add the decimal in the thousandths place, the third place from the right.

40. C: Divide the numerator and denominator by 14.

Additional Bonus Material

Due to our efforts to try to keep this book to a manageable length, we've created a link that will give you access to all of your additional bonus material.

Please visit http://www.mometrix.com/bonus948/fsag5mathwb to access the information.